Breach of Trust

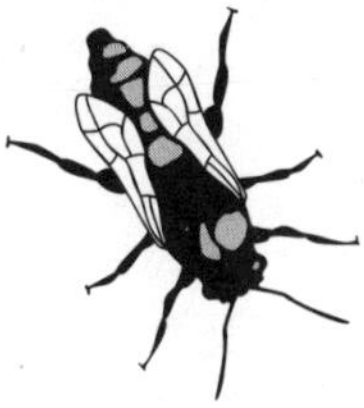

Breach of Trust

My Harrowing Years as a Foster Child in the Care of the British Columbia Ministry of Social Services & Housing

Gloria May Biron

IRON BEE PRESS

Published by Iron Bee Press
Suite 1003, 1557 - 4th. Avenue
Prince George, British Columbia, Canada V2L 3K1

Phone: (250) 612•9283
E-mail: GloriaMae.com@telus.net

CANADIAN CATALOGUING IN PUBLICATION DATA

Biron, Gloria May, 1972 -
Breach of trust

ISBN: 0 - 9687089 - 0 - 0

1. Biron, Gloria May, 1972 - 2. Foster children--British Columbia--Biography. 3. Abused children--British Columbia--Biography. 4. Foster home care--British Columbia--Biography. I. Title.
HV887.C32B72 2000 362.73'3'092 C00 - 910583 - 2

CREDITS:

All Photographs from the Biron Family Collection
Interior and Cover Design, Last Impression Publishing Service
Printed and bound in Canada, Friesens, Altona, Manitoba

Dedication

EARLY drafts of this book were written as a catharsis and as part of a process of healing. This story is dedicated to my children, Bruno and Brittany, and to my family of origin: my father Larry, my mother Helen, my brother Ronnie, and my sisters Mary and Ruth.

It is also dedicated to every other family unit who has experienced being broken asunder when children are unnecessarily or prematurely apprehended and taken into alternative care. In publishing my story and in giving voice to my experiences, it is my hope that I can give a voice to others—the silent majority—who were similarly abused and assaulted while in the care of either a ministry of a provincial government responsible for family and children's services, or a government-controlled agency, such as a children's aid society.

By illuminating the dark and destructive nature of my own experience in the child welfare and foster care system, I hope I have set a course of action that others might follow. Among those who read this story, I know there will be some who will feel they are reading about themselves and their own lives.

If, while in care, you have been or are presently a victim of any kind of abuse or assault—physical or sexual, emotional or psychological—I hope my story gives you the courage to tell yours. Whether your experience of assault or abuse was new—meaning you were victimized for the first time while you were in care—or a repetition of something first experienced elsewhere, is simply not relevant. To be apprehended and removed from your original family unit because of assault or abuse, be it real or suspected, only to be abused or further abused in an alternative, approved-as-safe child care resource, be it a foster home or a group home, is a complete travesty of justice. It represents a betrayal that calls for the prosecution of those responsible.

If government support for families and child protection services are ever to be significantly improved, we must challenge and support those responsible for implementing policies and procedures. They need to work with greater diligence towards the creation of a system that increasingly focuses on prevention through education; to strive for early, more accurate identification and diagnosis of potential client needs; and to make appropriate interventions when it becomes clear that any sort of intervention is required. Decision makers and service providers must be judged not only to be professionally competent case managers, but also to be accountable for personal decisions and actions that affect the lives of the children in their care.

I also hope that this account of my years in foster care will provide greater understanding of and insight into the present state of family and child welfare services in British Columbia, which is probably no worse nor markedly any better than any other province or territory in the nation. Eyes and ears, hearts and minds, once opened, can never be closed. None of us can ever ignore that which we have become aware of, so I hope you will use whatever understanding and insights you gain from reading my story to help make the system of social welfare—wherever you live—more open and transparent and effective.

In his anthem, "The Future," Leonard Cohen sings, "There's a crack, a crack in everything; that's how the light gets in." If my story helps to break the silence and collusion that often surrounds what happens to children when they are made wards of the court and taken into care, then I will have achieved something for the greater good.

To other victims of assault or abuse while in care, I sincerely hope my story will help you to find the courage to "get cracking" on your own account.

Gloria May Biron
Prince George, British Columbia
March 2000

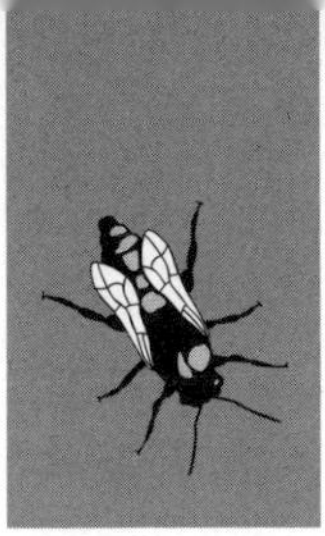

Acknowledgements

My heartfelt thanks to those who underwrote the production and printing of this book, not just for their financial support but for their belief in me and my reasons for "going public" with my story: the pursuit of social justice, the collective good, the safety and well-being of children and families, and for harmony within all families.

To all those who have helped me personally in the interim years, I would like to express my deep gratitude—to my parents, my siblings, my own children, other relatives, and my close friends, including a few of my former foster parents—you have helped me reclaim and enjoy a sense of security and well being.

For editorial, design, and pre-press skills, I would also like to thank those who worked on the production of this book.

A special thank you goes out to other former "wards of the court" for your generous encouragement and support. Many of you also had less than positive experiences during your own time in care; some, like me, experienced abuse and assault. In hearing your stories and by witnessing your sorrow and pain, I relived my own and was graced with your trust, giving me the courage to find my own voice. While not all of us can or need to "go public," I have chosen to do so because I can, and because some cannot presently take that step. My voice is also your voice until you can find your own.

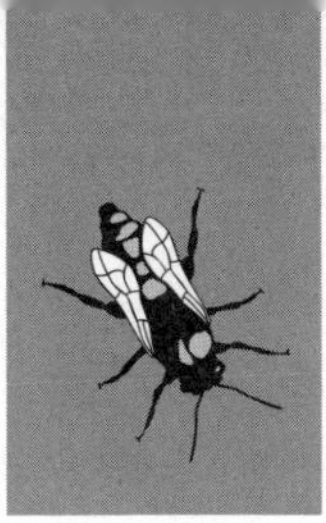

Disclaimer

WHILE the events described in this book are true, all names—other than those of the author and the members of her immediate family—including the names of child care resources, have been altered to preserve anonymity and avoid prejudicing ongoing legal proceedings and civil settlements; therefore any alleged or assumed resemblance between persons living or dead can be considered entirely coincidental.

Contents

1

Life at Home

March 1972 - December 1985

I was born in Sault Ste. Marie, Ontario, on March 19, 1972, my parents' third child. Their second child, my sister, died at the age of three from Tay-Sachs disease, shortly before I was born. So there were just the two of us—my brother, Ronnie, who was seven when I was born, and me. My mother, Helen, said I was a breath of fresh air for all of them, a new life in their world.

The loss of a young child can tear a family apart, but my parents wouldn't let that happen. Instead, they put their trials and tribulations behind them and moved on, holding my sister forever in their hearts. My father, Larry, moved us across the country to British Columbia, where we could start a new life.

My mother is amazed at my memory of the details of my life, but I swear I can remember travelling through the Rockies for the first time when we drove out to B.C. I was about eighteen months old, and I can remember looking out the window and not understanding why our car did not just fall to the bottom of the valleys. The grades were extremely steep. At times we were looking straight down.

We settled on a small acreage just north of Prince George, but still within the city limits. Soon afterwards, my mother had another baby girl, my sister Mary. She and I are exactly twenty-seven months apart. I can remember waiting for my mother to bring her home from the hospital.

Because our family had grown, we had to move from our little farm to a bigger place and we did that when I was two and a half. I remember walking from room to room and going from cupboard to cupboard, saying goodbye to every inch of the house with tears in my eyes. I was heartbroken to leave that house and move into town. This was the first "saddest day of my life."

When my sister Ruth was born, a year and a half later, my brother was disappointed. He had wanted a baby brother rather than another little sister who would just bug and tease him. Now it would be three against one. As funny as he was, and as much as he loved to tease us, he became distant from us as he got older. Seven years is a large gap between children. He had his own life with his friends and a world full of goals and dreams.

I know we three girls were quite a handful for our parents. We were fiery little things, full of life, laughter and love. Sometimes we fought like crazy. Our parents would probably say that an alley-cat brawl didn't compare with our fights, but we didn't let our fighting undermine our relationships with each other. We were always the best of friends and closest of playmates.

I can honestly say we were happy children. Of course, there were the normal family ups and downs, but there was never anything we couldn't work out. We could always forgive and, of course, forget. I don't ever recall having much to worry about, except when it came time to bring home our report cards. Our parents never expected us to be perfect in school, but they did expect us to do our best. If they felt we hadn't done as well as we could have, we would have to stay home after school and study three evenings a week until the next report card showed improvement. This happened to me in grade four, and I swore I would make sure it didn't happen again. I hated being grounded.

I never questioned my parents' love for any of us. Our mother was a very kind, softhearted, gentle person. Sometimes she was probably too softhearted with us girls. Our father was always playful, funny and very generous with all of us. He was also very strict, but in a positive sort of way. If we ever talked back to our parents, we would be sent to our room or grounded for a whole day. If you experience that once, you don't do it again! My father was also very clear with us about his dislike of drugs, alcohol and smoking. We were not even to try them. Once, when Ruthie was nine, she was caught trying a cigarette with her friend and she got grounded for a week. As a result of his "lectures," when we reached our later teens and were introduced to "dope" or drugs of any kind, we really weren't interested. Ronnie hung out with a good crowd. He was always into physical fitness and, as a varsity wrestler throughout his teen years, he had no interest in either drugs or in getting into trouble. Basically, we were all pretty good kids when we were growing up.

As generous as they were, our parents never spoiled us materially—only with love. There were loads of hugs and kisses in our house and there was always time to play, whether it was a game of *Snakes and Ladders* or just chasing each other around the house to tickle one another. We girls loved sneaking up behind our dad and surprising him. The shock of suddenly being caught and tickled would send him flying into the air. We thought this trick was great fun!

I also remember every gift my parents ever gave me or made for me. There were presents like the kissing doll and scaled-down microwave oven—which really worked—gifts I had dreamed about for a long time before getting them. And then there were all the little, incidental things, like a chocolate bar. Even a new toothbrush every few months was like a gift. We didn't need a special occasion, birthday or an anniversary for giving a gift. We appreciated everything, even if the treats were things we had in the house all the time, like pop and ice cream. It was always fun and exciting to have them.

I can recall we did a lot of memorable, fun things together as a family. I remember camping and fishing trips to lakes all over Canada. Many of the most wonderful family vacations we had were at Grassham and Vivian Lakes in B.C., and at Tilley and Echo Lakes in Ontario, and on Lake Superior. Occasionally, when we were at home on a weekend, we might be woken up in the middle of the night and be taken into town to Shakey's Restaurant, where we would sing and eat Shakey's fries, pizzas or chicken. This was the greatest thrill, and it has left me with memories I will never forget.

We used to say that my mother was a cleaning freak because she always liked to have a clean house. She was a bit of a night owl, so she would stay up and clean after we were in bed. She said it was the only peaceful time available in which to get the cleaning done. And she didn't believe in spring-cleaning. Every day was like spring in our house, and Mom was forever shampooing the carpets or washing the ceilings. She was also a great cook, and I loved watching her bake or cook while my father was at work. Her specialty was homemade bread and pastry for pies. I studied her technique, watching what she did with every ingredient and how she turned the spoon in the mixing bowl. I memorized where she would set the dial on the stove and which pots and pans she used for everything she made.

At the age of five, while my parents were out and my brother was babysitting, I baked my first batch of bread—twelve loaves of bread and three dozen buns. I had watched Mom so often that I was sure I knew how to do it, and I wanted to surprise her. I thought I was ready to try the big recipe I had memorized by watching her bake. Today, I realize that the recipe my mother used for her bread was at least triple the size of the regular recipe.

I was halfway through my bread making when my parents arrived home. When my mother saw what I was doing, she got very angry. She wasn't angry because she thought I was going to make a mess, as I had learned from her to clean up as I went. But she *was* worried that I didn't know what I was doing and that I would waste the last of her ingredients for making bread. "Just let her do her thing, Helen," I heard my father tell her quietly. "Go and lie down."

Dad didn't tell her that I had practiced for weeks with very small amounts of ingredients. When dad looked at me and smiled, I knew that he hoped this much larger recipe would turn out. I could feel his confidence in me, and I could see it in his smile.

Later, when my mother got up to start dinner, she was shocked at how well my bread and buns had turned out. They rose and baked up to twice the size of the ones that she usually made. I still don't know if it was my tiny hands that kneaded the dough, or the excitement, confidence and thought that went into the mixing, rising and kneading that made the bread such a success. Even today, my mother tells me how badly she feels for getting angry with me over this episode.

From the time I was little, I was different from most other girls of my age. By the age of nine, I didn't want to play with Barbie dolls anymore. I was more interested in making my own money. My parents opened a bank account for me and showed me how to deposit my money into a savings account. At first, the bank required one of my parents' signatures whenever I made either a deposit or a withdrawal. Dad would plan special trips into town, in order to take me to the bank. When the bank saw how actively I was depositing money into my account but rarely taking anything out, they told my parents they no longer needed to accompany me. When I wanted to withdraw money, they said my mother could just phone the bank and let them know I wanted to make a withdrawal. What I liked best about earning and saving money were the discussions with my parents about what I could do with some of my income and the sorts of things I could save for. I loved the independent feeling I got from having my own money, and I was prepared to work for it.

It was the early eighties, and lots of people were wearing jewelry—bracelets and necklaces—made of leather and beads, and many designs incorporated pieces of fur and feathers. I thought I could make some nice jewelry using the rabbit pelts Dad and Ronnie brought home from hunting. Sometimes they would come home with a dozen rabbits, which represented a lot of fur for me to work with. Behind my parents' backs, I would work the furs into jewelry and other items. I made rabbit-toe earrings, bangles of fur, key chains, and hand-warmers—little fur muffs. I'll never forget the first time I went door to door with my creations. People were just grabbing things out of the baskets and, after three hours, I went home with over $600 and a head full of ideas for new rabbit-fur creations.

I was so excited! I couldn't wait to tell my parents. However, I had neglected to tell them what I had been doing with all of the rabbit fur. When I walked in the door, put all my money on the table, and told them I had sold the furs from the rabbits, they were quite angry with me. Later, after I had explained how I had made things using the furs, they were full of questions and encouraged me to carry on. I had given our phone number to some of my customers and, over a period of one year, I made about $3,000 on my fur creations. As well as saving money, I always bought gifts for my parents and my brother and sisters. The money I earned also gave me the freedom to start picking out some of my own clothes for school and helped to pay for courses I was interested in, like babysitting and modeling.

I started babysitting casually at the age of ten. By the time I was eleven, when other babysitters my age made only $1.50 per hour, I was making $7 to $10 per hour as the most highly recommended sitter for major hotels in Prince George. I really loved looking after children. Apart from going to school, babysitting became my full-time job. For about six months, I had a contract, which paid me $220 a week. After school, I would go to look after a two-year-old boy, clean house and prepare dinner for the mother, who worked shifts sorting mail for Canada Post. She would come home for her dinner break and to check in with me, see how we were all doing, and then go back to work. When she came back at midnight, I would go home and look forward to the next day. The little boy got so used to having me look after him that the mother had difficulty leaving him with any one else, even her close friends, so I could have a day or two off. I continued this job, Monday to Friday, spending weekends at my own home, until the family moved away, but they provided me with great references for my work.

Soon afterwards, at the age of twelve, I began to pursue my dreams of a career in modeling. I attended model search-events where there would be talent scouts and agents from around the world, and usually hundreds of girls who, like me, hoped to be selected as models. At the time, I had long hair, long enough that I could sit on it! Because of this, I was often chosen for modeling hair fashions. I ended up being selected for a variety of modeling assignments, and in 1986 - 87, I was picked to appear in the Sears catalogue. With what felt like early success to me, my main goal in life became one of graduating from all the modeling courses that were expressly required by those agencies representing professional models. The courses were expensive and, as my parents couldn't afford to pay for them, I used the money I had earned from jewelry making and babysitting. Knowing it would help with my posture and movement, I also enrolled in jazz dance and ballet lessons. I felt that a career in modeling would open the door to all my dreams.

I wasn't a child who got into trouble a lot at home, but when I did I would get a scolding, or I would be grounded or lose privileges or access to favorite toys. Usually a scolding, combined with a light smack with the back of the hand, was enough punishment for us girls. Unfortunately, my father had grown up in a family where the belt was used as discipline. He didn't use it often, and I don't remember him using it on my sisters and me before I was eleven. If we got the belt, it was because we had been fighting, and we would all get it at the same time. When Dad did take out the belt, it was a long time before we would do anything so serious as to provoke him to take it out again—and so these events were infrequent. We had good memories! Sometimes all he had to do was mention the belt in order to keep us in line.

I know I always preferred any form of discipline other than being grounded, but it was never our choice to make. As I always had something on the go—babysitting, school sports or just bike riding with my friends—when I was grounded, I couldn't do any of these things. I wasn't even allowed to use the phone to call friends or go babysitting.

From the age of twelve through thirteen, my whole life was about modeling, babysitting and school sports. As more boys at school seemed to like to look at me and, as Dad became aware of this, he also became more strict with me. From the beginning, he had made it very clear to me and to my sisters that we would not be allowed to date until we turned sixteen. When Dad realized it wasn't just the boys my age who were looking at me, but older ones too, he wasn't about to change his mind on the matter. Even then, I fit pretty nicely into a tight pair of Levi's or Keda jeans and, because of my modeling experience, I had learned how to apply makeup. I used to wear darker lip-gloss than most other girls did and this just set me further apart as different from most of my peers. As a consequence of my extroversion and blossoming womanhood, the level of tension at home increased and the channels of communication started to close down. When this happened, I began turning to people outside of my home, including a teacher who had befriended me.

Over several months, I became closer and closer to my teacher, Mr. McIntosh, an attractive, single, thirty-year-old man. Before I knew what was really happening, we had become best friends, calling each other and hanging out together at every possible opportunity. Bernie became my confidant about my frustration with my parents, and he always looked out for me.

I began spending more time with my teacher, including visits to his home, and he would talk me into staying later and later, past my weeknight curfew of nine o'clock. Not knowing where I was, my father would be worried sick. Sometimes it would be as late as ten or even eleven o'clock before Bernie would finally drive me home, always being careful to drop me off a few houses away from my own. When this happened almost every night throughout the week, it made my father very angry. In response, he used the belt on me far more frequently, and began dictating what I could and couldn't do with my life, and who I could and couldn't see, or be friends with at school.

Although Dad assumed I'd been staying out late with friends, he became convinced that some of my friends were boys and he would lecture me on the kinds of boys I was to stay away from—boys who were into dope and alcohol. Some of my peers were already experimenting with these things, often financing their purchases by stealing from their parents. I thought my dad was becoming crazy. I wasn't even hanging out with boys. I wasn't interested in them yet, and I felt embarrassed that my dad was talking to me about this stuff. I felt misunderstood and overprotected. It was easier to talk with my teacher, who appeared to want my friendship as much as he wanted to be a friend to me.

My father was worried about the changes in me and felt I was becoming secretive about what I was doing and where I was going. When my mother would get into a discussion with him about me, it would soon turn into an argument. Dad thought he should become even more strict as a parent, and use the belt more frequently with my sisters and me, even if our chores were left undone or not done properly. He started grounding me more for these same reasons, and I was receiving more frequent "lickins" with his belt. If my mother attempted to intervene and prevent my father from being so physical in his approach to discipline with any of us and not be so strict or overly protective, he would become frustrated with her and tell her not to interfere. When he fought with my mother, there were times he would become extremely abusive, sometimes lashing out at my sisters or me as well.

I recall feeling that perhaps times were hard for my parents, just as they were for lots of other people at that time. British Columbia was in a recession, and the economy in Prince George was pretty bad. In addition to Dad being laid off from time to time, I thought that maybe my parents were having personal and financial problems—problems that we didn't know about. I remember frequent arguments between them, especially at night after we had gone to bed. They would be up discussing financial matters, and those discussions, too, turned into arguments. My father seemed to be under stress a lot of the time, and I guess his worrying about me didn't help.

2

The Apprehension

July 1985 - December 20, 1985

By the summer of 1985, I was spending a great deal of time with Mr. McIntosh. I had become so close to Bernie that he said he wanted to marry me as soon as I turned sixteen. While this was very flattering to me—in the way that any young teenager would be flattered to think that a man would like to marry her—it also didn't seem either quite real or proper. Ours was not a sexual relationship—I was only thirteen years old! It was true that I had confided in him a great deal and had grown quite dependent upon him. Bernie knew about the arguments at my house, and he knew my dad used the belt on me. Sometimes, when Dad used the belt on me, I was left with awful bruises on my legs. At these times I would never participate in school sports that required me to wear shorts. Although I couldn't see it myself, it was apparent to Mr. McIntosh that our family unit was breaking down.

Bernie began to phone me at home. He would suggest that I lie to my parents and tell them I was taking the dog for a walk so I could be free to visit at his house after school. In his classes, he treated me differently from other students—more like a woman than a child. He had also become quite possessive of me and of my daily routine—my life. He would phone me at about four o'clock each afternoon to ask me to come over to his house. He made weekend plans for the two of us. He bought me expensive gifts of clothing and makeup that he wanted me to wear. He played me the music he wanted me to listen to. He wanted me to cook for him at his home. Once, he became quite enraged when I had a few inches trimmed from my hair. He even introduced me to his mother!

While I liked Bernie and trusted him and enjoyed the way he made me feel, I really had no idea of his true intentions for me, despite his proposal, until much later. Even then, I found that reality hard to accept. Looking back on it now, I can't understand how I could have been so naïve. Our friendship had become much more meaningful to him than I had ever dreamed it would be. While I was beginning to experience his level of control as an invasion in my life, I was also unaware of how caught up I had become. Many times, I had to be deceitful with my parents to preserve the secrecy of our friendship. I recall feeling very confused. Oftentimes, I didn't understand myself when I was around Bernie, but the feelings I had for him were not what I would have described to be love—as I now know it.

Unfortunately, my parents didn't immediately become suspicious of Mr. McIntosh until he started to do things like send Mom and Dad flowers with attached notes, in which he told them how wonderful it was to have me in his class, or how well I was doing, and all of the other things parents like to hear about how their children are doing in school. My parents did express concern and had meetings with the school principal and actually talked to Mr. McIntosh about his behaviour with me—which they believed to be inappropriate. By the time these interventions occurred, it was already too late. Levels of trust between members of my family—between my parents and me—had sunk pretty low.

Disappointing my parents was the last thing I ever wanted to do, but the circle of confusion in my life left me believing that my parents didn't trust me anymore. I didn't understand that they were only trying to protect me from some of the harsh realities of a world that I believed had been good to me.

One wintry night, early in November, when there was lots of snow on the ground, I ran from the abuse at home. I was not wearing shoes or winter clothes, and I ran into the arms of my teacher. Bernie was very afraid for me and tried to comfort me. He drove me home and was able to calm my parents, especially Dad, and persuade him not to punish me further that particular night.

The next morning, when I arrived at school, Mr. McIntosh was waiting for me and he led me straight into the vice-principal's office. The office was empty at the time and Bernie closed the door and put his hands around my neck. I recall him telling me how much he loved me, that he was going to marry me and would do anything for me. He bent forward to kiss my lips, but I put my head down, feeling as if he was taking advantage of me. Bernie kissed my forehead instead and told me that he had been so worried about me he hadn't been able to sleep the previous night. He then asked that I should trust him, and he went on to explain that he was going to make a call on the school secretary's phone and would tell me when to pick up the extension phone in the vice principal's office. A few minutes later, Mr. McIntosh called through to me from the next room and, upon picking up the receiver, I heard a woman's voice. She identified herself as a social worker and began asking me all kinds of questions about what was happening to me at home and how my father was disciplining me. She had already heard all about the bruises on my legs and asked me to explain to her, in my own words, how they had been caused. I realized that Mr. McIntosh must have already told her about my father's use of a belt to discipline my sisters and me, as he was the only one outside our family with whom I had ever shared such details. For the remainder of the conversation I proceeded to answer all her questions about the manner in which my father disciplined my sisters and me. After ten or fifteen minutes of conversation, when it seemed we were finished, this woman informed me she was coming directly over to the school to see me. She asked that I remain in the vice-principal's office and wait for her there, so I did.

A little while later, two women arrived at the school and it was quickly explained to me that, based on the information I had provided to one of them over the telephone, they had judged me to "be at risk and in need of protection" from my father. Apparently it was her legal duty, as a protection worker from Family and Child Services, to apprehend me and place me in protective custody, under the care of the Ministry of Social Services and Housing. This action would be temporary, pending a full investigation, which would be based on the report they had received from Mr. McIntosh, together with my own telephone disclosure. This social worker said she would also be apprehending my two younger sisters for the same reasons. It was Friday, December 20, 1985, the last day of school before the Christmas break.

By the time I was united with my sisters and we had been taken to the social worker's office, we three girls were feeling very scared, lonely and lost! The three of us were questioned all over again. On this occasion, all three of us were interviewed together, by the social worker from the child protection team, along with two RCMP officers. Collectively, they asked us a lot of questions about our family life and about our father, mother, and older brother, Ronnie. We answered many questions about our father's temper, his use of the belt, and the other ways we were disciplined by our parents. We told them about his verbal abuse towards us and our mother. They also asked questions about our brother and his behaviour toward us. I told them that Ronnie used to tease us a lot, but it was all just in good fun, sibling rivalry—annoying but essentially harmless and typical brother-sister behaviour.

Both the protection worker and the police asked each of us whether our father or our brother had ever sexually abused us. Of course, nothing like that had ever happened to any of us, and that is exactly what we told them. They expressed collective surprise when they learned the words we used when we referred to either the penis or the vagina. All of them stated that they had never heard anything like these family terms before. In our family we had grown up referring to the vagina as *the prune* and the penis as *the brute*. While we had no explanation to give for where the term *the prune* had come from at that time, I knew the story behind the term we had adopted when referring to the penis. Our father and brother had developed the habit of watching wrestling on the TV together, and they especially liked a wrestler who was known as *The Brute*. When I was very young and we were still living on the farm, I got very upset one day when I saw the rooster mating with the hens. I didn't know what the rooster was doing, and so I ran to ask my dad. He laughed and said the rooster was like *The Brute*. Dad had said that the rooster was simply "bruting" the hens. After that, brute became one of our family's words and, as children, I don't think we ever gave it a second thought.

I recall the RCMP officers found my explanation and story rather amusing and, by the time I had finished, neither of them seemed particularly concerned. Once they were satisfied with their own questioning, the RCMP left us with the social worker. She continued to ask us questions about how our brother had played with us. When she asked us if Ronnie had ever touched our private parts, all three of us started laughing and said "No!" This was the truth—Ronnie had never done any such thing with any of us, at any time. As none of us could even imagine him ever doing that, we laughed again at her questions, thinking it was all rather ridiculous.

Although each of us had vehemently denied that Ronnie had ever touched us improperly, the protection worker kept asking us questions about how he tickled us. We had said that

Ronnie could and did sometimes tickle us so hard that we would lose control and wet our pants. When we would start screaming for him to stop tickling us, he would sometimes put a pillow over our heads and squish us just to make us mad. After we explained all of this, she asked whether Ronnie had ever had intercourse with any of us. Before that day, I don't think any of us had ever heard the word intercourse, let alone known what it meant. We assumed that the protection worker had summarized everything we had just told her into a couple of words, and that the word intercourse was one of them. We never did answer her with a yes or no. She didn't seem to require a yes or a no as an answer. "So, your brother had intercourse with you three girls," was what she said to us—and that is what she included in the statement and report that changed our lives.

3

My First Foster Home

December 20, 1985 - mid January 1986

THE questioning and interviews went on till around eleven o'clock that night. Afterwards, we were taken to McDonald's for dinner and from there to our first placement home. All three of us were scared, and none of us knew for sure, all the reasons for what was happening to us. We were also afraid of what our parents might be thinking. We didn't know if they were worried about us or whether they were simply going to be angry with us whenever we got home.

That first night, we were driven about fifteen or twenty kilometres outside of Prince George to a rural subdivision and placed in the care of a single mother, Shari-Lynn, with a young son, Tyler, around the same age as my youngest sister, Ruthie. Shari-Lynn and Tyler lived in a small, two-bedroom trailer home. None of us had anything with us but the clothes on our backs. I was wearing my indoor running shoes and had, somewhere between school and this foster home, misplaced my coat.

Shortly after we arrived, I received a phone call from my teacher. It was, by now, after one o'clock in the morning. Bernie had called me to see how I was doing, to tell me he loved me, and to tell me I was not to worry about anything. He also told me about how he planned to obtain approval from the Ministry for me to go and live with him. Afterwards, I realized that the social worker must have given him the number at the foster home —there was no other way he could have obtained it so quickly.

In some ways, I was glad to have heard from him. We were, after all, in a strange house with people we didn't know. I was also in shock. I couldn't believe that the social worker and social services felt my sisters and I were in danger and in need of protection from our father simply because he used to belt us when any of us did something he didn't approve of. We had been told that his use of the belt constituted physical abuse and that this was against the law. While I hated the belt, I had never felt that Dad abused us. I knew he loved us. I was so confused and scared, I really couldn't think about or concentrate on anything else.

That first night, Bernie continued to call every thirty minutes to an hour, well into the early hours. His speech was a bit slurred, and it sounded to me as though he'd been drinking and/or crying or perhaps both. Occasionally, usually whenever we sat around and listened to music, I had seen him drink a beer. Eventually, Shari-Lynn intervened and told him not to call again that night as we were all very tired and needed to get some sleep. Bernie didn't take heed and continued to call me all through that first night and regularly, though less frequently, over the next few days. We were not allowed to answer the phone and whenever Shari-Lynn picked up the phone and the caller wouldn't respond, I knew it was Bernie. Shari-Lynn finally got so fed up that she contacted our protection worker to have her put a stop to his calls or else, she threatened, she would see to it that he was charged with harassment.

Our social worker arranged for Shari-Lynn to take me to McDonald's the next day so I could visit with Mr. McIntosh. Shari-Lynn wasn't particularly happy about having to do this, but she took me anyway because Social Services had asked her to. Bernie and I were left together for about an hour and a half. He had brought me all kinds of gifts—makeup, romantic greeting cards, cassette tapes, and a ghetto blaster with the price tag still attached—$129! He had also bought some posters for me so I could start to decorate my new living space and try and make it more my own. Some of the posters included personal or inspirational quotes and phrases, such as "You're extra special"—sentiments which Bernie said he hoped I would find to be of some comfort as I adjusted to what had happened to me. One of the greeting cards had a handwritten note inside reminding me never to stop loving him.

All of his material gifts and expressions of love and affection made me feel very uncomfortable. I had never told him that I loved him and, as far as I could tell, I hadn't done anything to make him think that I felt that way about him. Bernie said the social worker had told him he wouldn't be able to see me or talk to me for a while, until things were more stable in our lives. He told me again that he was going to try and obtain approval and custody of me, so that I could go and live with him. In the interim, until that could happen and because he would not be able to contact me for a while, Bernie suggested that I should call him instead, whenever I got the chance.

About two weeks into our placement in foster care, Christmas had come and gone without recognition—since Shari-Lynn didn't put up a tree or celebrate the holiday at all—and we hadn't seen our social worker for days. Already feeling badly enough, it was a blessing not to be reminded that we were also missing Christmas at home. Since calls from Bernie had been stopped, we had also been prevented from phoning our parents or our friends, and we were also not allowed to receive any calls from anyone else. We weren't even allowed to leave the house without being accompanied by Shari-Lynn.

All of us were feeling lonely and homesick, and continued to feel confused, disoriented and scared. The foster parent's son, Tyler, had been acting in a sexually aggressive way towards Ruthie, who would be turning ten at the end of January. Tyler was forever touching Ruthie and grabbing her crotch. Ruthie repeatedly complained about this to Shari-Lynn. I cornered Tyler and told him to leave Ruthie alone, and also complained to Shari-Lynn. Her response was to become very angry with us and call us names—we were frequently told we were just a bunch of "spoiled bitches." Usually she sent all three of us to the bedroom we had to share.

Despite the fact that we entered care over the Christmas holidays, we all missed our parents terribly, and Ruthie really missed our Mom. As Ruthie became more and more depressed, she would cry all the time and ask to go home. Tyler would hide around corners in the trailer home and outside in the yard, laughing and making fun of her crying. Ruthie cried for days and it got worse instead of better as the days passed. Eventually, she stopped eating, and began to experience difficulty in breathing, perhaps because of her constant crying. Mary and I would lie in bed at night listening to her cry until she fell asleep sucking on a finger—something she hadn't done since she was a toddler. The silence would last only a few hours, as she would wake up and start crying again. All of this stress was starting to make me feel ill. Nothing I did seemed to comfort Ruthie, and it didn't help that Shari-Lynn was becoming frustrated. She would scream at Ruthie to shut up. When that didn't work, she yelled at Mary and me to get her to stop crying.

I had become very tired of her screaming at me and my sisters, especially at Ruthie. What nine-year-old wouldn't be upset if she was suddenly taken away from her mother? One day, I ended up screaming back at Shari-Lynn. I told her to shut up and stop shouting at us. I also told her to leave us alone. When my sisters saw that I was losing it, they became even more worried and upset. During this particular episode, Ruthie became almost hysterical. I hadn't realized that my calmness had helped keep both her and Mary from reaching their breaking point. Up to this point they had both been depending on me. When I lost control, they realized that I was just as scared, worried and frustrated as they were.

Shari-Lynn became verbally and physically abusive toward us. She was constantly smacking Ruthie across the face, and she threatened to use the belt on all of us if Ruthie didn't stop crying "I want my Mommy" all the time. Shari-Lynn locked Ruthie in a very small room, not much bigger than a closet, and told her she couldn't come out until she snapped out of it. Knowing that my other sister, Mary, had a phobic fear of the dark, she locked her up in a dark, tiny closet as well. She then locked me in her room and put a chair up under the doorknob, telling me I would get the belt if I even thought of acting up. This sort of treatment was extremely confusing for all of us. How could Social Services tell us we needed protection from our father because he used the belt and then put us with this witchy-woman who threatened us with the same sort of discipline? As I sat in Shari-Lynn's bedroom, I could hear both of my sisters screaming and crying—one terrified of the dark and promising she would do anything for Shari-Lynn if she would just let her out of the closet, and the other screaming for me and my mother.

This sort of separation and isolation happened to us more than once and would continue for a few hours, sometimes from one to two o'clock in the afternoon or from seven to nine o'clock at night. I can still hear Mary crying, "Please, I'll do anything. I want to be with my sisters." Finally, Shari-Lynn would go to the room, scream at Mary to shut up, and tell her she would let her out if she could quiet Ruthie. Shari-Lynn told Mary to "beat the shit out of her" until there was silence.

Of course, Mary never intended to do that, but she agreed to, just so Shari-Lynn would let her out of the closet. Mary figured Ruthie would likely settle down and just be happy to see her. As events unfolded, this was not to be. Ruthie continued to scream and cry about wanting to go home. Mary was clearly afraid that Shari-Lynn would continue to lock her back in the closet. Frustrated with the situation, Mary started to hit Ruthie and pull her hair in a vain attempt to try and get her to shut up—but she was unsuccessful.

After a few more days of this sort of behaviour, Ruthie snapped and, while screaming hysterically at Shari-Lynn to leave us alone, told her that she was a witch and a "miserable old bitch." After Ruthie said this, Shari-Lynn grabbed her by the hair and dragged her outside. Shari-Lynn had been threatening to take Ruthie outside and wash her face in the snow, and it was apparent that she was about to make good on her threat. The temperature that day was somewhere between ten and fifteen degrees below zero and there was quite a bit of snow in the yard. Ruthie was screaming for me to help her, but both Mary and I were in shock. We didn't know what we could do. It was as if all of us were paralyzed. Tyler stood by too, watching all this unfold, and simply laughed. Shari-Lynn bent to the ground, picked up a big piece of frozen dog excrement, and proceeded to force it into Ruthie's mouth. As if this wasn't enough she continued by pushing Ruthie's face into the snow. She sat on Ruthie and, still holding her by the hair, rubbed her face in the snow until it was all scratched from the ice crystals. To Mary and me, it seemed that Shari-Lynn wasn't ever going to stop. She was a big woman and it was obvious that her weight would be squashing Ruthie, and making it difficult for her to breath.

When we saw that Ruthie had stopped struggling, I think both of us thought Shari-Lynn had killed her. We were both crying, and Mary started screaming at me to help Ruthie. Something inside me snapped too, and I ran towards Ruthie. I tried to rip Shari-Lynn's long hair out in an attempt to unseat her and get her off my sister. I don't know where all my strength came from, but I grabbed her and dragged her by the hair about five feet away, hoping that Ruthie would get up and run, but she didn't. Her body was twitching when I knelt down to help her. Mary was still screaming blue murder! Ruthie's eyes were rolling up in their sockets and the frozen dog shit was still partly stuck in her mouth and throat. I cleared her mouth, yanked her up to her feet and shouted at her to run. Ruthie tried to stand, but she kept falling, just like a dog I had once seen after a car had hit it.

I couldn't believe what had happened. I was still so terrified—and angry—that I ran back to Shari-Lynn and attacked her again. "Look what you've done to Ruthie!" I shouted at her. Mary was screaming for me to go and help Ruthie who was now standing but taking unsteady little steps, and obviously very much in a daze. I'll never forget how confused she looked. Her eyes were so big they looked as if they would pop right out of her head.

It was cold and we were cold and, as there was nowhere else for us to go, we had to go back inside. We went to our room and sat close together on the bed, frightened because we did not know what Shari-Lynn might do to us next. We felt sure that something worse was going to happen. We overheard Shari-Lynn make a call to our social worker and tell her that I had become a big problem and would she find an alternative placement for me as soon as possible. Shari-Lynn told the social worker that she had no control over my sisters as long as I remained with them. When I heard this, I assumed the social worker would figure out that this woman was being abusive towards us, and this caused me even more confusion, because Shari-Lynn had been much more abusive towards us than our father had ever been.

As soon as Shari-Lynn had finished her phone call, she came to our room, knowing full well that we could not have helped but hear her end of the conversation. "If you think I'm mean, you haven't seen anything yet!" she said, smiling at us. Shari-Lynn told us how nice she was compared to many other foster parents, and then told my sisters they should be thankful she was letting them stay with her instead of being sent elsewhere with me. All of us started crying, especially Ruthie, who reiterated that all she wanted was to go home to Mommy.

The following day, our social worker, Wanda, arrived to take me elsewhere and it was clear that she was angry at having to do so. She acted as if it was an inconvenience, and she wasn't interested in anything I tried to tell her about Shari-Lynn and how she had treated us. When I left my sisters, I had a knot of fear and worry in my stomach. If the Ministry could take us away from our parents and place us in foster homes—where we were abused verbally and physically—I was convinced that they could do anything they wanted with us, and no one would ever know about it. It crossed my mind that it would be possible to even be killed while in the care of the Ministry, and conceivable that no one would ever know the real story. For quite some time after I was removed from this foster home, I was so confused and concerned for the safety of my sisters, I became convinced that my sisters might die if they stayed with Shari-Lynn for very much longer. Social Services had explained to us that we had been apprehended because we were in need of protection from our father—because he was verbally abusive and used the belt as a means of discipline. The truth was that we had been subjected to much worse abuse during our first three weeks in care—and this in a childcare resource, a foster home, approved by the Ministry as safe and where we were supposed to be protected.

4

Foster Home Number Five

mid January - mid March 1986

WHILE I had only been in care a few weeks, it felt like forever. Time seemed to pass very slowly. To have been kicked out of our first foster home and separated from my sisters was punishment enough. I was further punished by not being permitted to contact Ruthie and Mary—even to say hello and find out how they were doing. I missed my parents constantly. I missed the security and peace of going to sleep at night knowing they were down the hall. No matter what happened, deep down I knew that my parents loved me—loved us all. Until then, I don't believe I had ever taken time to think about that. Like most children, I think I had simply taken their love for granted—as implicit—because Mom and Dad were always right there, showing their love for us. Now that I had been separated from my sisters, and every member of my family had been taken away from me, I was actually able to appreciate what they represented—we don't know what we've got till it's gone!

In retrospect, I realize I was also scared to death without them. I must have decided that from this point onwards, for my own protection, I should be very quiet and keep to myself. Initially, I was surprised that no one seemed concerned that I wasn't attending school, and that no one had suggested I should be attending. As I didn't want to initiate anything that could be seen as troublesome or provocative, I didn't ask any questions.

I was afraid of what might happen to me if I were to become a nuisance to the Ministry and to the provincial government.

On being removed from Shari-Lynn's home, I was placed in several overnight and two-day emergency placement homes until such time as Wanda could find a long-term placement for me. These temporary homes were quite nice, and so were the people who cared for me. However, I formed the opinion that perhaps they were nice because it was easier for the caregivers to be that way, knowing that I would be with them for only a short time. When that time finally came, my next long-term placement proved to be another home outside of the Prince George bowl, about the same distance out as Shari-Lynn's place, but in the opposite direction.

Wanda drove me out there, but she didn't stop long enough to introduce me to the new foster parents. She just walked me to the front step and, when they answered the door, she handed them some papers and told them she would call them at the end of the week. It was apparent that she had talked with them before she dropped me off, as they knew everything about me. These new caregivers, Martin and Mavis, also knew I was not allowed to contact my parents, my sisters, or my teacher, Mr. McIntosh. Martin and Mavis were an older couple and looked very stern. I soon found out that their personalities and attitudes were congruent with that first impression.

As soon as I had settled in and they had showed me my room, they made me take a shower. I remember the soap was awful and irritated my eczema. My bedroom was in their basement, alongside another bedroom, which was occupied by another foster child named Jenny. She was younger than me, about the same age as my sisters. The couple's grandson, Eric, was also staying with them. He was nice, and about the same age as Jenny.

At first, I thought Jenny was a bit odd because she would look at me in a strange way or just walk away from me. I noticed, too, that Eric behaved as though he was afraid of or perhaps intimidated by both Jenny and me. After my shower, Martin and Mavis sat me down and outlined their house rules. I was told that as a foster child I was a bad influence on their grandson. Therefore, I was not to talk to him, and he was not to talk to either Jenny or me, and we were not to encourage him to do so. Jenny and I were not allowed to speak unless we were spoken to, and if we didn't do as we were told, we would get our heads smashed together. At mealtimes, Jenny and I would be told what we could eat and how much food we could put on our plate—even though they knew that I couldn't eat certain foods because of my eczema. If we didn't do as we were told at mealtimes, both of us would spend the rest of the day in our rooms with nothing else to eat until the following day. We were also not allowed to talk while we were alone in the same room. If either one of us broke any of these rules, both of us would be disciplined. Martin and Mavis emphasized that if we were caught "poisoning" their grandson's mind we would spend a very long, cold day outside with no food. These people claimed they were devoutly religious. They were members of the Salvation Army Church in Prince George.

About 1:30 am on the second night, Mavis came to my room, woke me up, and dragged me out of bed. She brought me to the top of the stairs and told me to sit there and not move. She went and sat beside her husband on the couch around the corner. They began talking to me and I remember feeling my level of anxiety grow—not just because of what they were saying but because of their tone of voice. I guess my social worker had told them about my relationship with Mr. McIntosh, because they began running me down for it, calling me a stupid bitch. My parents had been right to "strap" me, as they put it. They told me that Mr. McIntosh had been trying to obtain the Ministry's approval to adopt me, or at least become my foster parent so he could have me live in his home. They also said the

RCMP were investigating him for his behaviour towards me throughout the school year—both during and outside school hours. They said charges were pending against him.

Apparently, my parents had found his romantic cards and letters in my bedroom, and these were now in the hands of the Ministry. After thoroughly searching my room, and going through what few belongings I had with me, Martin and Mavis found two more recent letters Bernie had given to me just before and soon after I was placed into care. Martin and Mavis told me they would be handing these over to the police "ASAP." They said the teacher was a sick and disturbed man, a child molester, and I was an idiot if I believed otherwise. They also said my parents were going to prison for ten years for the way my father treated me, and that this had all come about as a result of my relationship with my teacher. They assured me that if they had a daughter like me, they would break her back and make sure she would never walk again.

My response to their moral dressing down was to burst into tears. I was crying so hard I could hardly breathe, but that didn't stop them. They kept right on with their tirade, even after I begged them to stop. They claimed that I had lied to my social worker, that Mr. McIntosh and I had together fabricated lies about my parents, and that I must phone my social worker in the morning and admit that everything I had said about my father was untrue. If I didn't do this, they promised I would have a very long, cold day ahead of me to straighten out my head. (In other words, I would have to stay out in the cold until I admitted that I had lied when I said my father had been abusive towards my sisters and me.)

I was really confused by this. As I understood it, foster parents were supposed to help me. The Ministry had taken me into care because of reports that I needed protection from my father's method of punishment. I now believe it was part of a game. During that first telephone conversation at school and throughout the interviews that followed, when RCMP officers had been present, I had only told the truth and nothing but the truth regarding my father. Despite the fact that I had never lied about anything, Martin and Mavis were trying to convince me to the contrary. I reflected long and hard about everything I could remember saying to the protection worker, all the answers I had offered to her questions, trying to remember if I had said anything that could be seen as a lie.

I thought if I could remember something I had said that wasn't true, maybe that would prevent my parents from going to prison. No matter what—and I kept telling Martin and Mavis that this was so—I hadn't lied about a thing. I didn't have to lie. I was talking about my parents, after all, and no matter what they'd done to me, I still loved them. I knew my father wasn't perfect. He hollered a lot at my mother, my sisters and me, and I knew it was wrong for him to use the belt to punish us. Nevertheless, the last thing I wanted was for them to be charged or convicted. Any way I looked at it, I knew I had only told the truth and, if telling the truth was a sufficient reason to put me in care, then there was nothing more I could do, given my present predicament. I had no idea that telling the truth would have led to the profound consequences my parents now had to suffer. All of this was running through my mind as these foster parents were calling me names and insisting I must admit to Social Services that I had lied. I was crying hysterically. I felt so confused, scared and alone that to die at that moment would have been like a gift from God.

While these people were responsible for and could see my state of mind, they did nothing to comfort me, and finished up by yelling at me to get out of their sight. I asked them to help me back downstairs, as I was afraid to go back to bed alone. Being fearful was a nightly occurrence and had been since my apprehension. My level of stress and anxiety did nothing to promote easy sleep, and more than ever, this night, I recall feeling so afraid, it seemed like I was going crazy. I told Martin and Mavis that I didn't feel good about being alone and asked them if they could just talk to me for a while until I calmed down, as I was having difficulty breathing.

They simply got angry because I wasn't obeying them by getting out of their sight quickly enough. They called me a bitch—a name they often used during the time I was with them. Martin eventually got up from the couch and started pushing me down the stairs, telling me to get moving unless I wanted my back broken. He said something like that should have been done to me a long time ago. This really frightened me. He was so angry that I was afraid he would hurt me, so I moved quickly to my room.

I was so scared that sleep was the last thing on my mind. I thought of running away, but who could successfully run away from the government? If I did run away and these people caught me, I thought they would probably kill me. I imagined how they would do it, where they would ditch my body, and believed that they could accomplish this without anyone ever knowing. In retrospect, I realize this sounds irrational but I was still only thirteen and still quite naïve about much of the world, adults, social systems and their use and abuse of power and authority.

I remember trying to decide if I should stick to the truth about my father as I had reported it to the protection worker and the police, or recant and say that I lied to prevent them from going to prison. I thought about the risks I would face by changing my account of life at home. If I were to do this, perhaps I would be sent back home. I had no illusions that my father would have changed much in the space of a few weeks. He would probably be even more angry with me and, if later on, I really required protection from him, maybe no one would believe me. Such a situation might provide my father with even more free reign to continue to be verbally and physically abusive towards my sisters, our mother and me.

From that second night, at bedtime, I was afraid to be in the dark, so I used to leave a bedside light on. There was a Bible in my room, and I opened it up to the book of Job and read from it for the rest of the night. I started thinking that if there were a God out there, he would know that I had told nothing but the truth about my father, and he would help me. I continued to read about Job and how his faith in God was seriously tested. I didn't think about much else.

The next day, Martin and Mavis came to my room to call me for breakfast. Before allowing me to sit at their table, they asked me to tell them if I had made any decisions about "our conversation" the night before. Because I hadn't slept, the conscious part of me had almost forgotten about the conversation, and their ultimatums, so I was caught off guard by their further questioning. I had decided not to lie to anyone. I would tell the truth about my father. But all I could say was "No." When I said this, they told Jenny and I to put on our shoes. Thinking that it would cause me to feel sorry for her and change my mind, they made her suffer along with me. Martin and Mavis called us "bitches" and told us to get the hell out of their house. It was very cold outside, but they had made it clear we would be outside all day if that was what it took for me to change my mind. After staying up all night reading the book of Job, I decided to look at this as though it was the first of many plagues. I didn't care if we froze to death.

Being outside and away from the two of them gave Jenny and me our first chance to talk freely. Jenny said she had been with Martin and Mavis for quite a while and had repeatedly complained to her social worker about how they were treating her. Her worker would never listen to her. In fact, whenever she had complained, her worker would simply report back to the foster parents and repeat everything Jenny had shared in confidence, and she would end up being treated worse than ever. Jenny felt social workers generally wouldn't believe you whenever you reported that things were not going well. They always behaved as if you were making things up because you didn't like a particular placement and wanted out. Jenny thought the only way out was to kill herself. It really frightened me to think that these people could get away with doing whatever they wanted and no one else seemed to care. I was beginning to believe that as bad as it was in my own house when my father was angry, it was a hell of a lot better than living in physical and mental torment in foster care for the rest of my teen years. Still, I decided I wasn't going to give in and give Martin and Mavis the satisfaction of knowing they had been able to convince me to change my story and say that I had lied.

After a couple of hours, we were no longer able to feel our faces, or ears, or our hands and feet—we couldn't even talk anymore. From the warmth of the house, Martin finally yelled at us from the back door, "You bitches get in the house now!" We were sent to our rooms. Both of us were so cold and I started to cry with the onset of the pain that often accompanies rewarming of the extremities. Rewarming caused pain I cannot accurately describe. I only know I never want to experience it again. To this day, I cannot contemplate being outside in the winter unless I know I can easily get inside somewhere where it's warm; otherwise I experience a sense of panic that I will get so cold I will have to go through rewarm pain again. Friends and family say I routinely keep my house so hot they often find it difficult to breathe.

Jenny and I finally warmed up, but I experienced sensitivity and throbbing in my fingers, toes, ears and cheeks for several days afterwards. My face was particularly raw, and my lips cracked and bled, and my finger joints were a bit swollen and sore. Jenny felt the same symptoms. While outside, we had so valued being able to talk to each other that we attempted to continue once we were back inside the house. When Martin and Mavis heard us talking, they intervened and knocked our heads together. We didn't immediately know why they were doing this until they reminded us of their rules. I think when you're that cold, your mind slows down and it takes longer for things to register. My third day was neither happy nor productive. Jenny and I had not been given breakfast or lunch and we spent most of the day alone, in our respective rooms—until supper time. Neither Martin nor Mavis said anything more about their wanting me to change my story.

In the days following our outside punishment, Jenny's lip bubbled up into a blister that eventually began to bleed. Because we had to share cups, I ended up developing a cold sore as well. With my face already so raw from the cold, I developed further cold sores all over my face. I can still remember standing in front of the mirror, watching the cold sores break and the fluid run down my face. I was sure I was going to have to spend the rest of my life ugly and scarred because these people wouldn't take me to a doctor. While Mavis wouldn't take us into town, she did seem desperate to find something to help heal my face. I think they were worried that the doctor would figure out that we were being treated badly. Plague number two is how I saw it.

Jenny and I were never allowed to lock the bathroom door while we were bathing or showering, and both Mavis and Martin seemed to think nothing of walking in on us while we were bathing or drying ourselves. I began to think that Mavis sent her husband in just so he could see my body. I would scream and grab the shower curtain and wrap it around myself when he came in. "Oh, don't be ridiculous!" Mavis would yell at me. There was never a specific reason for him to enter the bathroom. I only remember him opening the door and standing there staring at me as I scurried to cover myself up.

Days rolled into weeks and I had neither seen nor heard from Wanda since the day she dropped me off. With only my ghetto blaster and the Bible in my room, I was bored to death. Relief from boredom happened when Eric would sometimes sneak in to visit me. When his grandparents caught him in my room listening to music with me, they took my stereo and drowned it in the bathtub. After this incident, Mavis would find any excuse to come down on me and would threaten to "break my back." On one occasion, her own daughter was visiting, and she simply stood behind her mother and said, "Do it Mom, break her back. We'll say it was self-defence."

As Martin and Mavis were active members of the Salvation Army Church, they would drag us along with them whenever they attended church meetings. Occasionally they would be invited to stay on after the meetings and service and have a few drinks—they were drinking hard liquor—and when this happened we wouldn't get home until the early hours of the morning. The hypocrisy of this kind of behaviour disgusted me. Jenny and I were forced to sit around and watch them get drunk in a church. Inevitably, "a few drinks" always turned into "a few drinks too many." The man who did most of the talking during the meetings was always touching my behind. I tried to prevent this by moving in between the piano and a wall and from there, I would watch him go around and feel up anyone else he could—even the married women. One night, I threw up in the church because I was so tired. Jenny started crying, and asked Martin and Mavis, for the umpteenth time, if they would please take us home. Eventually we did go home, but not before it suited them.

Finally, one day, out of the blue, Wanda called me. I was really puzzled by what I learned from her. As mean as Martin and Mavis had been towards me, they had reported all sorts of nice things about me to my social worker. They had even told Wanda what a pleasure it was to have me in their home! After I finished speaking with Wanda, she asked me to hand the phone over to Mavis. I later learned from Mavis that Wanda had called to set up a time for all of us to go into her office and meet some people who were opening a new group home called the Northstone. The new contract service suppliers wanted to interview each of the prospective children-in-care candidates before making a final decision about their suitability for a group home environment.

I recall being very excited about the possibility of leaving Martin and Mavis's home, if for no other reason than I had begun to think that maybe Jenny was right when she had said that the only way out was to kill yourself. When Mavis told me why Wanda had called, Jenny had been within earshot and I immediately saw disappointment in her face. Jenny had been with Martin and Mavis a lot longer than I had and now I was being given an opportunity to leave, and she would have to face living with them on her own again.

The day of our appointment with the new group home parents arrived. On our way into town, Martin and Mavis couldn't warn me enough and continued to threaten me, saying they would break my back or starve me to death if I said anything to Wanda about their treatment of me in their home. They kept telling me they would do these things and I should take them seriously. I was scared. I felt certain they would find a way to be present for this meeting to make sure I kept my mouth shut. When we arrived at Social Services, Wanda called me through to a meeting room behind the front reception counter. She asked Mavis and Martin to come back for me in half an hour. Mavis turned quite pale and both she and her husband just glared at me as Wanda closed the office door.

The group home parents, Caroline and Lawrence, were waiting for us in the office and, in Wanda's presence, it only took one question from them for me to break down and tell them of my experiences with Martin and Mavis. They asked me how I liked my present foster home and I told them the truth about Mavis and Martin and how they had treated Jenny and me. As I told them how I felt about Martin and Mavis, and how they made me feel, I started to cry. Then I asked Wanda why she had not visited since she had dropped me off at the door, or even phoned to see how I was doing. Wanda didn't attempt to answer. In fact, she behaved in exactly the same way as Jenny had described *her* social worker had done—as though I was making it all up. I left this meeting thinking that Caroline and Lawrence had believed me.

When Martin and Mavis returned to collect me, I was shocked that Wanda just sent me on my way. It was as though she hadn't heard a word I had said. On my way out, Wanda told me the group home wasn't due to open for another month. When they saw my disappointment at the thought of another month with Martin and Mavis, Caroline and Lawrence spoke up and said they would call me from time to time to check in with me so they could get to know me a little better over the phone. I didn't know that this was their way of telling me they believed what I had told them and that they would do what they could to look out for me. I went home with Martin and Mavis, feeling a bit despondent and quite unsure about how much longer I could tolerate their harsh treatment.

When we arrived home, Jenny was very sad and quiet. I really didn't know what to say to her, as I couldn't ever say what I wanted to say whenever Martin and Mavis were within earshot. Not long after we got back in, Jenny asked to be excused, telling Mavis and Martin that she felt sick and probably shouldn't come to supper because she felt like she might throw up. Mavis and Martin let her stay in her room. After supper, I had an odd feeling that I should check up on Jenny. On impulse, I slipped off down to her room. I knew that part of the reason why Jenny was feeling bad was because I was leaving, and I was feeling kind of guilty about that.

When I knocked, Jenny didn't answer or open her bedroom door. When I tried the door and opened it, I saw her hanging from the light fixture in the ceiling. Somehow she had managed to take a belt and, while standing on a chair, loop one end around the light fixture and electrical cord and the other, in a noose around her neck. The chair was lying on its side where she had obviously kicked it away from under her. As soon as I saw her, I screamed for Martin and Mavis to come and help. The hanging didn't work out as Jenny had obviously intended. She was choking—her lips were blue and her skin looked mottled, but she wasn't dead. I ran and grabbed hold of her, pulling her down. When I pulled on her, I yanked the light fixture right out of the ceiling. I was told later that if the ceiling hadn't given way, I could have killed her by breaking her neck. It was awful and I was terrified.

By then Martin and Mavis were there. Martin carried Jenny like a baby and went upstairs with her and laid her out on the couch where they sat with her for a while. I know they called an ambulance and that Jenny went to the hospital, but most of the details of what followed are hazy. I think I must have been in a state of complete shock. On the way out the door, Jenny looked at me and said quictly, "I'm outta here."

Over breakfast the next day, Martin and Mavis tried to convince me that Jenny's suicide wasn't serious. She'd only tried to hang herself to get attention. Then they accused me of helping her plan her suicide, saying it was something we had schemed up together. While this was ridiculous, I didn't really care anymore about anything either Martin or Mavis said. I was just happy that Jenny was out of their home and that nothing worse had come out of her suicide attempt and that it had not caused her any permanent physical damage.

I still have nightmares about Jenny. I see myself walking into her bedroom as she's hanging there and, while she looks half-dead, she is also looking back at me. I run towards her but she keeps getting further and further away from me. No matter how I try, I cannot reach her to either hold her up or pull her down before it is too late. Usually, I wake suddenly, overwhelmed with nausea, feeling in some way that I failed her because I couldn't reach her in time.

Sometimes I wonder what would have happened if I hadn't acted on my feeling that I should check up on Jenny, or what would have happened if I had checked up on her just five minutes later? Would she have been dead? Would she have become just another statistic for the Ministry? Perhaps the incident would have been hushed up and forgotten, like so many other things I experienced during my time in care. The system probably would have written it up in such a way as to minimize the episode and dismiss Jenny as just another "problem child." It's easy for Social Services to say such things about any child in care—and build a picture that effectively discourages anyone else from looking further into the background of those involved, to try and discover what would make a child so desperate as to attempt suicide.

As good as their word, Caroline and Lawrence called me to find out how I was doing, but I was never allowed to take these calls alone. Mavis would always stand right next to me whenever I was on the phone, glaring at me to make sure I never said anything about what was going on in their house. It didn't take Caroline or Lawrence very long to figure out that I was unable to speak freely or answer all their questions completely.

It was less than a month after our first interview, and quite unexpectedly I received a phone call from Caroline and Lawrence to inform me they were on their way over to pick me up. The Ministry had agreed to let them take me earlier than originally planned—and get me out of Martin and Mavis's home. I was so happy! I didn't care anymore about hiding my feelings from these people. This sure put a cramp in their style. I could tell they were concerned about their reputation when they started asking me if I knew why the Ministry was moving me out of their house earlier than planned. In a few hours, I was all set to go, and Caroline and Lawrence arrived to pick me up. Martin and Mavis had the nerve to ask me for a hug goodbye—no doubt to try and make themselves look good in front of Caroline and Lawrence.

Even though Caroline and Lawrence seemed nice, I still felt lost, confused, scared and extremely lonely. I couldn't get used to being surrounded by strangers. After all I'd been through in the last month and a half, every night had become a sleepless experience. I felt guilty, and blamed myself for what had happened to my family. These feelings robbed me of any sense of self-worth. My spirit was broken. I had no one to turn to for compassion or reassurance, and no friend I could rely on in this new world. I was not well physically and felt sick often. I missed my sisters terribly. I needed their company and I wanted those playful times back again. I just wanted to be with them so we could share our thoughts and cares the way we had in the past. If it hadn't been for all I had learned in the many nights I spent reading the Bible, I probably would have done something as rash as Jenny. I thought about suicide many times, whenever the confusion, the guilt and the loneliness became more than any child-in-care should ever have to bear.

5

The Group Home

mid March - June 1986

FOR the first weeks I was with Caroline and Lawrence, I lived with them in their own home as we all waited for the group home to open. It was much easier to be with them than it had been at the last place. They were so nice, at first I thought they were faking it. They also had two beautiful children, Kurt and Melinda. One was still an infant and the other about two years old. We all got along just fine. Because Caroline and Lawrence were so nice to me, I wanted to do everything in my power to please them so things would always stay that way.

Immediately after moving into their home, I became very ill and vomited almost daily for weeks. I was very confused that these people who had initially been so nice to me gradually began to change, acting as if I was pretending to be sick just to get attention. I couldn't understand why they didn't take my illness seriously. Caroline kept telling me I just needed to get some fresh air, so she would send me out for walks. I still hadn't returned to school and, because I was feeling ill, I didn't always want to be outside. With few options, there was nowhere else for me to go but to the local shopping mall. Whenever I was in the mall, and I felt nauseous, I remember the embarrassment I felt when caught short and people saw me dry-heaving. When I began to heave, I felt so weak that I had to stop and find a place to sit down. Once I sat down in the middle of the aisle in a drugstore. Mostly though, I remember how helpless I felt. I was supposed to be able to trust Caroline and Lawrence, but nothing I could do or say stopped them from misjudging me. They appeared to believe that I was lying and faking my illness. Only after I had lost a lot of weight—I was only 103 pounds to begin with—did they take me to see a doctor. Caroline told him she was sure my constant sickness was simply attention-seeking behaviour that had gotten out of hand. After the doctor examined me and took blood tests, it was discovered that I was suffering from Rubella (German measles). Rubella is quite contagious, and I learned that I had been a danger and could have infected others whenever I had been out wandering about the mall. After being sick for weeks, I was finally able to get better with prescription medications.

Shortly after the group home was opened and we all moved in, I was registered at a new school to continue in grade seven. Not long after we moved in, the RCMP came to see me and question me about my relationship with Mr. Macintosh. Apparently, the police had questioned other girls about him. In all, they talked to about one hundred girls, and close to forty of them described their relationship with him as being similar to mine. In fact, a social worker for the school district had issued an alert about him as a result of his previous relationship with another girl.

While my parents had informed the Superintendent of School District #57 about my involvement with Mr. McIntosh, Wanda was able to prevent my parents from attending either of the two hearings that were held regarding Mr. McIntosh's relationship with me. Later, I learned that my parents had been informed that Wanda had defended Mr. McIntosh, claiming him to be "one of the last good Samaritans." According to a representative of the RCMP, who said the force wanted to lay charges against Mr. McIntosh (but couldn't because of a lack of evidence), "it was just a matter of time before he crossed the line with Gloria." The police were so sure of the results of their investigation as to be able to state, in the presence of my parents, that they felt their "investigations led them to believe that he was setting Gloria up for intercourse." I am sure Bernie must have been grateful to Wanda for defending him and, in the end, I heard he received six months probation with no permanent criminal record.

I also received news that my previous foster parents were being investigated and that their fostering privileges had been revoked. I was glad to hear that no other children would have to experience what Jenny and I had been through while in their home—but this wouldn't do much for all of the foster kids who had come and gone before us and who had also lived with their abuse. It's sad that, even after hearing the complaints from the foster children living in their home, the Ministry did not look into the complaints or take them seriously until a little girl almost died. After Jenny had tried to hang herself, the Ministry still placed another foster child in the home. I often wonder how many other kids continue to be abused or do things like attempt suicide because no one will listen to them or believe what they might say about the care they receive while in Ministry-approved childcare resources. If you are a child in the care of a provincial ministry or Children's Aid Society, and you are not in your social worker's good books, it is my experience that you are even worse off than you ever were in your own, natural family home. Basically, in foster care, you can quickly wind up being on your own without help from anyone who has the time to act as an advocate for you or for long enough to serve your best interests.

After living in the group home for a while, I was beginning to feel very close to Caroline, who was really like a big sister towards me. Nevertheless, every night, when I went to bed, I worried about the events of the day and especially when I had done something that would make Caroline or Lawrence angry with me. I would lie awake for hours, going back over each minute of the day in my mind, reassuring myself, trying not to worry, so I could go to sleep. Over time, I became obsessed with doing anything and everything I could, simply to please them and win their approval. I feared for the day when they might decide they didn't want me at the group home anymore and would send me somewhere else. I wanted desperately for them to understand me. I now realize that it was just wishful thinking on my part, to have imagined that anyone would be able to fully understand the feelings and traits of someone whose spirit had been broken, unless they too had experienced this for themselves. While I watched other foster children come and go from the group home, there were some who, like me, appeared to be staying indefinitely, with no plans of ever leaving until they reached the age of majority (19 years) and were discharged from care to independent living.

While life was better for me at Northstone, things weren't going as well in my new school. At first, everything seemed fine, but I felt some teachers were picking on me. From the moment I walked into class, my homeroom teacher made comments about my hair or makeup. Even though he didn't specifically refer to me by name, the class knew who he was talking about, and they would all look back at me and laugh. I felt that he was singling me out because he was aware of the investigation conducted on Mr. McIntosh—via the School District grapevine.

When public health nurses came to the school to check students for lice, my homeroom teacher stood in front of the class and said I should go first. "Lord knows, you're probably going to take the longest," is what he told me. Of course, the whole class started laughing at me. I wondered if his behaviour came from some place of blame, that somehow he held me responsible for what had happened to Mr. McIntosh, even though he didn't know all of the circumstances or my side of the story.

I wasn't the only student in my class who was subject to ridicule by the teacher. There was a Sikh boy who, according to his tradition, didn't cut his hair and wore it in a bun. Despite his refusal to take his hair down, the teacher forced him to do it. When the class saw how long his braid was, everyone, including the teacher, started laughing. The boy stormed out of the class in tears.

Because my teacher made fun of me, other kids in my class followed his example. While he teased me in the classroom, the other pupils obviously thought they had free reign to tease me outside of the classroom. Things at school gradually got worse. The first time I mustered up the nerve to approach his desk and ask for his help, he hollered at me, "Sit down! That ain't going to work with me!" I had no idea what he was talking about at the time. All I knew was that I had missed more than two months of school and had to work hard to catch up. As an adult, I now understand the implications of his comment.

This teacher was really quite cruel, and things got to the point where I would regularly burst into tears and run out of his classroom. When I came back, I would really be in trouble, because my leaving gave him just one more thing to criticize and condemn. Things came to a head the day I screamed at him, in front of the class, "Just leave me alone!" I left the school and ran all the way back to the group home.

By the time I arrived, Caroline had already heard from the school and that I had been suspended for talking back to my teacher. I really didn't care anymore. Before Christmas, prior to being apprehended, I had been a really good student, able to tutor other kids. Now I was a student in need of a personal tutor to help me through the rest of the school year—and that is what I did.

After my experiences in foster care, I desperately needed to reclaim my dignity and my sense of self-worth. I had always been a free spirit, but now I needed help. I started to rely more and more upon Caroline. I needed to be around her, and I needed her to be my friend. I felt so indecisive. She seemed to understand my state of mind and my sadness. Whenever I was with her, whether we were just talking or shopping together, I felt like she was my friend. It was my dream just to have a friend I could get to know, trust, and confide in. I had been cut off from my world of loved ones—my family and closest friends—for far too long.

6

The Sexual Assault

July - August 1986

DURING my stay in the group home, the Ministry met with Caroline and Lawrence and asked them whether they would accept another foster child, an older teenage boy. Because they trusted me, Caroline and Lawrence came to me and warned me that the boy was a known sex offender. They asked me if I would help them to watch over their own two children, Kurt and Melinda, as the boy was known to molest other children regardless of their age. I didn't mind helping to look after their children, but I was confused. Some of the girls who were living with us in the group home were already victims of sexual abuse. Why would the Ministry place a known sex offender, especially one who had abused younger children, into this situation? Shortly after this guy arrived at the group home, Jenny also came to live with us. She was already a victim of sexual abuse.

Without prejudice, I think Ray was the kind of person most people would refer to as a bit of a geek. Caroline and Lawrence would have to work hard in order to get him to take a shower at least once a week; otherwise he might never have showered at all. He appeared to live in his own world and spent nearly all of his spare time working on his computer. In this regard, he appeared to be really quite smart.

Soon after his arrival, he started to harass me sexually. He was forever asking me if he could touch certain parts of my body. He wanted me to show him what it felt like to neck with someone and asked me to show him how to practice using his pillow. This sort of interaction continued for quite some time and he became quite pushy about it. Caroline and Lawrence talked to him again and again, and went to great lengths to try and make sure he understood that he was to leave all of us girls alone. Their efforts only provoked short-lived changes in his behaviour; he didn't stop harassing me. Eventually, Caroline and Lawrence threatened him with a transfer to another resource if he did not refrain from pestering me. Caroline and Lawrence registered a number of complaints about Ray's behaviour towards me with the Ministry, but they were ignored.

Both Caroline and Lawrence were becoming quite concerned. They felt it was only a matter of time before the boy molested someone in their group home, and so they contacted the Ministry and asked them to find another placement for Raymond as soon as possible. While playing with Kurt and Melinda, Caroline had also caught Ray touching her children in a less than appropriate manner. Again, the Ministry ignored their request to have Ray removed from the group home. Still more time passed, and the group home parents finally called the Ministry again to let them know they had packed Ray's belongings, and he would be sitting outside on the front steps of the group home until a worker came to collect him. No one from Social Services ever showed up to take him, so he ended up staying on at Northstone.

After experiencing the Ministry's lack of response over their issues with Ray, Caroline and Lawrence decided they had to give up their privileges as group home parents. They reassured the rest of us that it had nothing to do with us and, while they were concerned about Ray, their decision had also been made out of a genuine concern for us as well as their own children. Despite their explanation, we were all disappointed by the news. Our group home parents didn't hide the fact that they had become fed up and disillusioned with the all of politics of the Ministry of Social Services and Housing and their haphazard execution of the policies and procedures governing contract care homes. Caroline and Lawrence told us they didn't want to be held responsible for any incidents in the group home arising out of the Ministry's lack of support.

There were just three of us CIC's (Children-in-Care) resident at Northstone at that time—Ray, the sex offender, Connor, a boy my age, and me—so the Ministry gave the parents permission to move the three of us into their own home until new group home parents were appointed. All three of us were given separate bedrooms in the basement. However, the room I was given was adjacent to one given to Ray. Each night, I tried to remain awake longer than Raymond; I felt I couldn't fall asleep before he did. Some nights this was difficult to achieve, as Ray would often stay up late working on his computer.

On one of the few nights I must have fallen asleep before he did, I stirred and half woke to discover my nightie unbuttoned and open part way. Ray had his head down by my crotch and was licking my vagina. When he realized I had woken up, he immediately stopped what he had been doing and moved quickly to the right side of my head, to whisper, "You're just dreaming, go back to sleep." In disbelief, I lay back down and closed my eyes for a few moments. I hoped I was indeed, just dreaming. Although I kept my eyes closed, I was, by now, quite fully awake, but it was as if I had been paralyzed. I continued to lie still, trying to convince myself that I was just dreaming and having this dream because I had been so afraid that something like this would actually happen. When Ray moved and started to suck on my breast, I realized this wasn't a bad dream—it was really happening, and my nightie was completely open when I flew off the bed, screaming.

I tried to make my way upstairs to wake Caroline and Lawrence and tell them what had happened, but Ray blocked my path. I tried unsuccessfully to wake up Connor, the other foster boy, then ran to barricade myself in my own room. I could hear movements upstairs, suggesting that Caroline and Lawrence had woken up with all the commotion. Ray had actually gone upstairs to Caroline and Lawrence's bedroom, woken them, and confessed to everything he had done. While Lawrence kept Ray outside until the police arrived, Caroline came and sat with me in my room. The police questioned me and took my statement, and this appeared to be the end of it, insofar as everyone else was concerned. I was not taken to see either a doctor or a counsellor immediately after the incident.

I thought I had learned what it meant to hate another person at the previous foster home, but it was horrifying to feel such hatred towards Ray—obviously a very sick and disturbed young man. I hated him even more intensely, knowing that he had done this or similar things to others. I was still a child and I had been exposed to something I couldn't ever have imagined. My innocence and naïveté around issues of sexuality had been stolen from me. At that time, I still wasn't completely cognizant that a man actually had to insert himself into a woman during intercourse and I knew nothing about concepts like oral sex. I wasn't ready to learn. I was too young. Now my introduction to sex had occurred in a premature, inappropriate, dirty, abusive, and unlawful manner. After learning "this stuff," I remember wondering if I would ever be able to live the rest of my life without feeling dirty or ashamed. I wanted to die. Later on, I recall being better able to describe my experience as a mind-body separation and some sort of mental or conscious refusal or denial to accept the physical reality of the situation. The night I was assaulted, it was all I could do to keep within myself. I felt humiliated and ashamed and embarrassed and soiled in a way no bathing or showering could ever wash off. Thousands of showers could not have washed away my sense of violation. Uncontrollable emotions ran through me. I was crying and screaming one minute, then laughing hysterically or shaking with rage the next. I also feared that, as a foster child, I would be labelled and become another statistic or case to be written up as a victim of sexual abuse. In a way, the chances of my being so labelled—and others like me—automatically increased when the Ministry knowingly placed a sex offender in the group home. When they repeatedly ignored the concerns and complaints—made by their own caregivers and service providers—to intervene and remove a problem child from a potentially explosive and destructive situation, it was only a matter of time. The Ministry played the odds and gambled with my safety. To be labelled a victim of sexual abuse then, is really a name the Ministry had already decided for me—and for others like me—when they allowed the abuse to happen.

For the remainder of that night, Caroline stayed with me. I felt as though I had levitated right out of my own body, enabling me to look down and listen to myself as my voice changed pitch, sounding just like it did when I was a little girl. I remember images wherein I was watching Caroline comfort me, trying to help me realize Ray had gone and that I was safe again.

The following morning, Wanda informed my parents that I had been sexually assaulted at the group home. Mom demanded to see me, so the Ministry arranged for her to meet me at Social Services. However, Wanda neglected to tell my parents that the assault had actually occurred in the basement of Caroline and Lawrence's own home, not the group home, and that I had been given a bedroom right next door to a known sex offender. Ray was charged and convicted and sent for a psychiatric assessment at a facility in the lower mainland. Under the Young Offenders Act, he was placed in another residential treatment facility where, I later learned, he molested a handicapped girl.

I continued to live with Caroline and Lawrence even though they were no longer running the Northstone Group Home. I

Ronnie, aged 7, with Gloria at 3 months, June 1972.

Ronnie 11, Gloria 4, Mary 2, Ruth 6 months, 1976.

Left to right: Ruth 6, Gloria 10, Mary 8, in 1982.

Mother Helen with Gloria 10 (behind), Mary 8, and Ruth 6 (seated), 1982.

Gloria, aged 10, 1982.

Helen and Larry Biron, 1984.

Gloria aged 13, shortly after being taken into care, 1986.

Gloria at 14, with her father, 1987.

From left: Ruth, Gloria, Ronnie, Mary and Larry, 1998.

Gloria with daughter Brittany 5, son Bruno 8, and dog, Angel, enjoy tobogganing, Winter 1999 - 2000.

Gloria and brother Ronnie, 2000.

Gloria and father Larry, 2000.

Gloria, with son Bruno 8, and daughter Brittany 5, 2000.

Gloria at 27, in a professional studio shot, taken in 1998.

lived with them in their own home, where I would clean and babysit for them. I liked doing this, it pleased them, and they trusted me with their own children. Kurt and Melinda liked me and maybe even loved me, and I certainly grew to love them as though they were my own brother and sister.

Now that I was fourteen, I wished I could just go home to my family so we could begin to work out the problems that took me away from them in the first place. My wish that this could be so was overshadowed by the further abuse, damage, pain and turmoil I had experienced since being taken into care, as well as that which had been brought on my family through false accusations. I realized that my being in care was not so much about my needing protection from the verbal and physical abuse of my father, as it was a political war and a power struggle between Wanda, representing Social Services, and my father. I was caught in the middle. Any sense of unity in our family had been destroyed. There was little left to work on or rebuild, and opportunities to repair the damage seemed remote.

Since I had come to live with Caroline and Lawrence, I had heard snippets of their conversations with my social worker. They believed that all my insecurities, loneliness, inability to trust and lack of self-worth could be attributed to my parents and the way they had raised me. I never heard them talk about all of the things I had been through while living in the care of the Ministry. I also overheard Caroline and Lawrence demanding that they be paid more money to look after me. They put these demands in writing as well.

> "We cannot, in good conscience, continue to accept Gloria as a foster child under foster care (as opposed to special care) rates, as Gloria is a young lady with immense confusion dominating her life.... Although Gloria has many lovely qualities and is, in many respects, a trustworthy, respectful and conscientious girl, she is a guilt-ridden,

> troubled young woman whose perspective of the world is becoming warped and naïve."

Another note from them reads:

> "Gloria was raised in a dysfunctional home, causing her to engage in defence strategies and coping mechanisms such as guilt, low self-esteem, guardedness, and inability to trust and an unclear sense of self-worth."

It truly hurt my feelings to learn how Caroline and Lawrence's ignorance and selfishness blinded them to the reality of my world and my experience.

The sexual assault changed my relationship with Caroline and Lawrence.The day after the assault, Caroline's tone of voice was different when she spoke to me, and so was her attitude toward me. I felt so ashamed, embarrassed and stupid about the assault that I tried as hard as possible to act as though it hadn't affected me. However, I did start wearing dark sunglasses, even in the house, because I found it difficult to look at other people directly—eye to eye. A few months prior to the assault, Lawrence had brought home a little dog for me, whom I had named Pippy.When it was just too difficult to be around anyone, I would simply take Pippy for a walk. After the assault, the first time I took Pippy for a walk, I dressed in a pair of jeans and a nice blouse. I paid some attention to my hair and makeup and put on some low white heels. As well as trying to make myself feel better, I was also trying to convince other people that I was more brave than I really felt. I didn't want anyone to think that I was upset by what had happened. On my way out the door, Caroline accused me of looking like a "slut" and asked me why I was taking the dog out dressed as I was. Her tone of voice would have sounded hateful to someone who didn't know her. Anyway, I acted as though I didn't hear her and walked out the door. She had hurt my feelings so much that I started to cry as soon as I was outside. I thought I had been doing a good job of covering up my feelings—by acting as though nothing had changed in my life.

As I walked down the driveway, a delivery truck pulled up and a man came up the driveway towards me, carrying a bouquet of flowers. Lawrence was famous for sending flowers to his wife and so I assumed they were for her. I took the flowers from the deliveryman and went back into the house. It wasn't until Caroline had opened the card accompanying the flowers that we realized they were for me and had been sent by some very close friends of Caroline and Lawrence. In sending me flowers, I realized these friends were only being thoughtful, but I had been so busy trying to convince everyone around me that I hadn't been affected by the assault, I had almost convinced myself as well. Suddenly, I felt like I was being assaulted all over again. I was confused. I didn't know how I was supposed to feel when other people found out I had been sexually assaulted or how I was supposed to react whenever they phoned to ask how I was doing.

Later that afternoon, Wanda showed up at the foster home. She seemed very upset about what had happened to me, but it sickened me to have to go through the sympathy ceremony again with her. I wished everyone would just stop talking about it. The Ministry had been warned many times by Caroline and Lawrence that something like this could happen. They had ignored all of these warnings until a sexual assault had happened to me—and only after the fact did they begin to show any concern. Wanda got annoyed about my wearing sunglasses while we were talking, and told me to take them off. It was as if she had asked me to take off my clothes. After we had finished talking, she stayed to talk to Caroline. I took Pippy for another walk. Wanda had already gone by the time I got back.

As I walked through the door, Caroline immediately began yelling at me to help her clean the house so she could start dinner. It was awful. The way she was treating me made me wonder if she felt I was to blame for being sexually assaulted in her home. Caroline kept saying to Lawrence, and other people—in front of me—how thankful they were that the sexual assault hadn't happened to one of their own children. To me, Caroline seemed to be saying that the assault wasn't really so bad because it had happened to me and not to one of their own children. Caroline remained short-tempered with me for weeks and weeks after the assault, and she was always criticizing me over one thing or another. At one point, Caroline realized what she had been doing and actually apologized to me, saying that she was the one who was acting like a fourteen-year-old, but this realization was short-lived and her frustration and annoyance with me simply returned.

Caroline would become upset at almost anything, and I felt that a lot of her anger was due to me. I began to hate myself for being sexually assaulted, and I actually believed that all the turmoil was my fault. One day, when we were outside, my dog began digging a hole in the flowerbed. Caroline grabbed Pippy by the head, shook her vigorously, and then threw her down. Thinking she was going to kill the animal, I screamed at Caroline to stop. When I picked my dog up, she made an awful, high-pitched yelping sound. Caroline told me the next time she caught the dog digging in her flowerbeds, it might not be so lucky.

Later the same day, I came into the house and left my shoes at the front door, just as the other members of the household did with their own footwear. As a rule, I had always been asked to take my shoes downstairs each time I came into the house. On this occasion, I had forgotten. As it happened, their youngest child, Melinda, chose to suck on one of my shoes. This threw Caroline into a rage, and she grabbed me by my throat and pushed me up against the front door.

Wanda had arranged for me to begin seeing Margaret, a counsellor with Mental Health. I think this was arranged so I would have someone else outside of the foster home with whom to talk about the problems I was now experiencing with Caroline. During the first few sessions, I talked freely with Margaret about how I was being treated, until I learned that Margaret was actually a good friend of Caroline's. After one appointment, I came home and Caroline proceeded to yell at me for telling Margaret about something that had transpired at the group home. It was then that I knew. Thereafter, for as long as my appointments with Margaret continued, Caroline would grill me about the session as soon as I got home. Caroline reminded me that she and Margaret were good colleagues and that she had a right to know if I was making her look like a fool. When I wouldn't tell her anything, Caroline would begin shouting at me. I told Margaret about all of this and how difficult it was for me. After one session with her, Margaret suggested I call her immediately, the very next time Caroline began shouting at me. When I got home, I went straight to my room, hoping Caroline wouldn't come and question me about the session. I had been in my room only a very few minutes when Caroline demanded to know what we had talked about. I stayed in my room. At the top of the basement stairs, there was a cordless phone in the hallway. When it felt safe, I took the handset and placed a call to Margaret's office in such a way that Caroline would be able to overhear. For about ten minutes, Margaret was able to listen as Caroline screamed at me in the background, outside my door. After reassuring me that everything would be fine, Margaret asked me to go upstairs and pass the phone over to Caroline, so I did that and, without saying anything, went back downstairs. From my bedroom, I could hear Caroline's sarcastic remarks in response to whatever Margaret was saying. Then everything went quiet. I remained in my bedroom until Lawrence came home.

Things didn't improve much. Caroline was forever making comments and putting me down. Once, after I had spent hours making myself a miniskirt, Caroline told me I couldn't wear it in the house or around her husband because he liked legs. I was invited to come along on a fishing trip with Lawrence, his father and Kurt. While we were fishing, Lawrence told me he would take me hiking sometime. I had such a good time fishing that I was really excited about the idea of going hiking. When I mentioned this to Caroline, she went crazy, telling me I had better not plan on doing anything like that until she first had a chance to go hiking with Lawrence—he was, after all, her husband, not mine!

Still, I was most thankful for the wonderful fishing trip. It had brought back many wonderful memories of holidays with my own father and family—hiking through the bush and forests to lakes where we spent many hours both fishing and camping. In my excitement, I shared my feelings with Lawrence, saying, "Gee, thanks for taking me out. You're just like my dad." Caroline and Lawrence both reacted strongly to this, especially Caroline, who yelled at me, "How dare you say such a thing!" She told me I was sick if I thought her husband was anything like my father. When I tried to explain what I meant, they warned me never to compare the two again. After this, Caroline told Wanda that I had a crush on her husband. My parents also heard this rumour and it made me feel humiliated and embarrassed. I couldn't understand why they would say such a thing. I only knew that Lawrence had been kind enough to include me in the outing and I appreciated it.

Shortly after all this, my Aunt Marlene and cousins Tommy, Andrea and Pamela came from the States to visit my family during the summer holidays. Because I was in care, my Aunt Marlene went to see Wanda to try and arrange temporary custody of me for the balance of their visit. Wanda granted approval for me to go home for the remainder of their holiday and I was able to see my family, including Mary and Ruthie. Both my sisters had remained in care as well, and were in other foster homes where they had also suffered physical, mental and sexual abuse. When the time came for my aunt to leave, Mary was afraid to return to her foster home placement. In *her* home, she was required to get up early every morning and "dig her own grave." No one in the Ministry had believed her, and so her placement in that home had been maintained. Mary had run away, but the Ministry simply had the RCMP pick her up and bring her back. Mary protested and although she told the RCMP all about the abuse she had suffered, it made little difference—they always took her back.

Even though I hadn't seen my Aunt Marlene and Uncle Leonard and my cousins for many years, Caroline kept calling my parents' place to talk to me. She asked me to come home to either babysit or help her clean the house, but I turned her down because my aunt always had plans for the day. On one occasion when Caroline telephoned, my Aunt Marlene took the call. She reminded Caroline that she was only here for a short time and that I was, for the balance of her vacation, in her custody so I could visit with my cousins. Aunt Marlene told Caroline I was unable to return to their home until the custody period and her holiday had ended. Caroline got very upset about this and started screaming at my aunt over the phone. I saw my aunt hold the phone away from her ear, and the rest of us could hear my foster mother yelling at us down the phone. Caroline persisted with my aunt, telling her that I had responsibilities to them in order to be a part of their household. My Aunt Marlene remained very calm during the conversation and the calmer she was, the more frustrated Caroline became.

I felt so awful. I was only going to be with my family for a few more days, and I was afraid of what would happen when I returned to Caroline and Lawrence's home. For the time being, I didn't have to worry about that. The next day, Caroline called again. She was cordial on the phone, but also very cool. Caroline told me that in order to be a part of their household, I would have to be available to them at all times. She felt that I wasn't as loyal to them as I should have been, so I was no longer welcome to live with them. She told me not to worry about my things. She had already packed them, and Wanda was on her way over to pick them up. I felt so used and betrayed that I cried for the remainder of my aunt's visit. Caroline broke my heart and she knew it. After having time to think about it, I realized that this was Caroline's way of getting even with me for whatever it was she felt I did to her.

Again my life was up in the air. I no longer knew if I was coming or going. For years afterwards, I was unable to explain to anyone how I felt about these events and their negative influence on me. I had no idea what was going to happen to me or where I was going to live. I felt completely lost all over again. All of the goals I had begun to establish for myself now looked to be impossible. It had been discussed and planned that I would likely remain with Caroline and Lawrence for the remainder of my teenage years, at least until I was nineteen. Until my aunt's visit, I had been living with them for almost six months, and it had taken me almost four months to relax with them and feel like I could be myself.

Once Aunt Marlene left, I would be on my way to yet another foster home. After all that had happened to me, I got really scared all over again. I had no idea where the Ministry was going to put me next or when it was going to end. While thoughts of suicide returned, I just knew I couldn't or wouldn't allow myself to be so stupidly selfish.

I found out that my brother, Ronnie, was being investigated for allegedly sexually molesting my two younger sisters and me. I thought this was just further trickery on the part of the Ministry to see how I would react and whether I would go back, change my original story, and admit what Social Services clearly suspected and believed to be true. However, as I later found out from my doctor, this investigation was genuine. After completing a medical examination of me, he reassured me that there were no signs that anyone had ever had sexual intercourse with me. When he said this, I spoke up. "Of course not," I said, "because no one ever has." Then he asked me why I had told Wanda that my brother had intercourse with all three of us girls. I remembered our original conversation with Wanda, and I remembered answering her questions regarding how our brother played with us and teased us. The doctor then told me that, according to Wanda, I had plainly said, in my own words, "My brother had intercourse with me and my sisters." This was an outright lie.

I found all these questions sickening, and I particularly detested being physically examined for verification of the allegations of my being sexually abused by my father and brother. I kept telling these people, over and over "NO! Neither my father nor Ronnie ever sexually abused me." When one doctor would examine me for sexual abuse and confirm what I had said, Wanda would arrange for a second opinion and take me to another doctor. I was getting fed up with having to strip naked every time I went to a medical appointment. After being examined by five different doctors and then, finally, my own family doctor, I refused to attend any further appointments for physical examinations. While the Ministry found my decision unacceptable, they also discovered how stubborn I could be. Out of frustration, and the fact that Wanda needed time to find a more permanent placement for the start of the new school year, they packed me off to a horse riding camp for the last two weeks of the summer.

I was lonely at this camp. I had so much on my mind and so many worries, and these put a damper on any fun I might have had. I spoke once again with Caroline, and we agreed to be friends. She said the family would come out and visit on my last day at camp and watch me demonstrate my riding skills, during our camps' Special Events Day. Knowing that Caroline and Lawrence did not like or get along with my own parents, out of respect for both, I did not invite my parents to attend the event.

The day of the show arrived, and I was really quite excited as I had a special spot in what they called the RCMP Ride. I had been looking forward to having Caroline, Lawrence and their children attend. I waited all day for them to arrive, and fretted about all the reasons why they might be late. At the last minute, just as the show was about to start, they still hadn't appeared. I decided to call them. I was very surprised when Caroline answered the phone. I reminded her that this was the day of the show. She asked me if my parents were there. I said, "No, because I knew you wouldn't like that." She giggled and told me they weren't going to show up either, and maybe now I would understand what it feels like not to be important. She reminded me of the day she had called during my Aunt's visit and had asked me to come home, to babysit and clean her house, and my aunt had told her, "No." Caroline had felt the same way then as I was likely feeling at this moment, because they were not going to show up for the camp's Special Events Day.

I couldn't hold back the tears, and I cried harder as it dawned on me that she had, all along, been planning to hurt my feelings just to get even with me. I was so hurt that I couldn't even say goodbye before she hung up the phone. The people who owned the camp were standing right by the phone, and they managed to figure out what was going on. They helped me calm down enough to go out and participate in the RCMP Ride—for myself, as they put it. They were very nice people. When Wanda came to pick me up and take me to my new foster home, they offered to let me stay longer as an assistant to the next group that was scheduled to start the following week. Wanda agreed because she felt the extra week would give me a little more time and space in which to pull myself together again before I went to my new foster home. I was really thankful to them all for giving me the extra break.

7

Another New Home

September 1986

At the end of my third week at the horse camp, Wanda eventually showed up to take me to my new foster home. The foster parent, Martha, was a single mother with a nineteen-year-old son, Andy. I wasn't allowed to have a bedroom upstairs in this woman's house, and her son had the only bedroom in the basement. Instead, Martha had made up a bed for me under the basement stairs, across from her son's room, and had hung a curtain to give me some privacy.

I really didn't care about where I was. It was enough for me just to have my dog Pippy with me, even though she wasn't allowed in the house. She and I had been through a lot together.

I hated this foster home after only two days. I was told to sanitize anything I touched, including the toilet, tub or bathroom sink. My dishes were soaked in boiling water from the stove after I used them, before they were actually washed. Each day, I was required to clean the house, working from top to bottom—this included walls, ceilings and light fixtures. If Martha didn't think I'd done a good enough job, she would stand over me to watch me do it again until she was satisfied. When there was nothing left for me to clean, she had me scrub the cement floor in the basement. I felt like I was a disease to her, and I didn't have the will to go through any more experiences like this. I also thought about Wanda, who wanted to make me a permanent ward. Was this the place she planned to keep me for the remainder of my time in care?

One day, when Martha went to town, I worked up the nerve to grab Pippy and run for my life. I remember thinking that because I was running from a foster home, I was also running from the provincial government. I imagined that they would send some sort of SWAT team out to look for me. For all I knew, a SWAT team might already be behind me. While running, I held Pippy so tightly that she barked and yelped at me. I was so scared that I ran through the bush until I got to the Fraser River. I must have fainted from the violent rush I was feeling because, all of a sudden, I woke to find myself on the ground with Pippy lying next to me. I couldn't see or hear signs of anyone else anywhere near me. I walked upstream, following the river until I reached a subdivision I suspected was an Indian reserve. Although I'd seen plenty of movies, I really didn't know much about life. I was extremely paranoid about anyone seeing me—afraid the police were looking for me—and here I was, sneaking around outside and between strange houses like a cat, but with my heart in my throat. I'd never run away from any foster home before and, now that I had, I felt little inclination to return. All I knew was that teenagers who were caught, were usually arrested and returned to the care of Social Services. And here I was, running from the Ministry of Social Services and Housing.

Pippy and I hung around undetected for several hours, staying a short distance away from the houses on the reserve, along the banks of the river. I thought of running home to hide with my own parents, but I wasn't sure if they still wanted me after all that had happened. Maybe they would turn me in. I had nowhere to go, and I felt like a criminal on the run. I thought of sneaking onto a train or something, going to another town, but I didn't have the guts to do that either. I was starting to get cold and began thinking that I didn't have the will to keep running and hiding, always worrying about getting caught. I talked myself into giving up and turning myself in—even if it meant going to jail! I picked up Pippy and started walking again. It didn't take me long to realize that I wasn't really surrounded by bush and that I was only on the outskirts of Prince George, a couple of miles at most from Caroline and Lawrence's home. I thought their home would be as good a place as any to turn myself in.

When I arrived at their door, everything seemed quiet. I rang the bell and was met by Caroline. I told her what I had done. She took me into the house and called Wanda right away to let her know I was safe. How stupid and shocked I felt when I found out that my great escape had not even been reported to the police. When I told Caroline about my fears—the SWAT team and going to jail—she almost died laughing. She made fun of me, talking to me as if I was stupid. I was embarrassed. I'd put all that fear and stress on myself for nothing.

It turned out that Wanda couldn't come to pick me up right away and, because I refused to go back to the place I'd just run away from, I had to stay the night with Caroline and Lawrence.

Ministry policy on runaways was quite simple. Whenever a runaway CIC was reported, the Ministry would simply have the child picked up by the RCMP. The police would do one of two things: either return the child to the foster home or hold them in custody until the duty social worker could collect and return the child. Even if the runaway complained of abuse in the foster home, the RCMP did not routinely conduct an investigation to verify the CIC's complaints or allegations.

8

Truth or Lies, I'm Going Home!

October 1986 - May 1987

THE next day, Wanda came to see me. She had with her a file almost an inch thick, the contents of which she said she needed to go through with me. Wanda told me that my period of temporary wardship was due to expire and she had to go back to court to apply for another extension if she were to keep me in care.

All I wanted to do was to return home to my parents. Wanda knew that, and yet she gave me all the facts about becoming a permanent ward of the court and described all the benefits, telling me that the Ministry would pay for my education right through to university level, if I ever chose to go that far. Knowing that I was extremely fond of modelling and dance training, she said I could alternatively elect to have them pay all of the costs for me to upgrade my skills in these areas. Wanda told me that the Ministry would provide the funds for whatever I wanted or needed—new clothes and other material things—at all times, which was not the case if you were only held in care as a temporary ward of the courts. Wanda then proceeded to tell me that the file she had contained all the information she needed for the judge of the court to grant an order making me a permanent ward.

Wanda said she wanted to go through with me, step by step, exactly what she was going to present to the judge, so that if and when he asked me about the information she presented to him, I would be able to answer all of the questions. Wanda told me that I probably wouldn't understand some of what she would say in court, but whenever I was asked a question, I should just answer yes to everything.

We were not long into the conversation and I was already feeling uncertain and increasingly uncomfortable about the direction we seemed to be heading, perhaps because I could sense Wanda's nervousness. I was shocked and confused to hear the first few things that came out of her mouth. She had been right when she said I might not understand some of what she was saying. I wasn't familiar with all of her vocabulary, but I could see that she had exaggerated many of the facts about my father. Wanda had constructed a history that implied my father had sexually abused me for much of my life. I quickly cut her off.

"I can't say that!" I told her. I then asked her if I had actually been kept in care all this time because she hadn't ever believed what I had said about my father. I had always believed my sisters and I were in care because he used the belt on us and because he was verbally abusive when he was angry. I learned that this wasn't the real reason why any of us had been kept in care. I now saw that something was very wrong, and the situation seemed very dangerous to me. My sisters and I had been kept away from our parents not so much because of what my father had done and what we said he had done, but because of what the social workers believed he had done. In my eyes, the Ministry had become the monster in this situation, not my father.

When I took exception to this dishonesty, Wanda became very angry with me. She told me that if I did not agree to everything she was going tell the judge when we attended court, she would send me home immediately. She reminded me how long I had been in care and away from my family—as if I had to be reminded. She asked me to think about things: What would my father be like today? Did I think he might have changed? How did I think he was going to behave with me, considering everything that I had put him through? I felt cornered. But I couldn't lie about my father to make him sound worse, much worse, than he really was. I honestly wonder sometimes how everything would have turned out if I had lied in court, and they had proceeded in their attempts to bring charges against my father. What Wanda had outlined with me as the basis of her presentation to the courts sounded very serious, especially about the sexual abuse.

I strongly believe that, somewhere along the line, the whole situation had changed from one where I needed protection from my father to one more focused on a political struggle between Wanda and Social Services and my father. My father obviously hated Wanda for taking us away from Mom and him, and he made her job and life very difficult by involving her superiors and the Minister's office in Victoria. He did everything in his power to intimidate her. Wanda responded by trying to do exactly the same thing to him.

When Wanda was unable to find a doctor who would corroborate her beliefs that my father had sexually abused me, she tried with all her power to find other things besides the physical abuse to throw at him. I remember hearing her tell a foster parent that she was going to have him investigated for fraud. She never followed through with that threat—she had no basis upon which to begin—but her interference cost my dad his job as a foreman. Wanda wrote to his employer and indicated that he was being investigated for fraud, stating she felt this was something an employer should be made aware of. After my father was laid off from his job, his employer told him about the letter he had received, but claimed that it had no bearing on his being made redundant.

Wanda's vendetta against my father was unrelenting. On one occasion when I had accompanied my parents to the Sears restaurant, we had been seated at a table and Wanda and her husband happened to be sitting close by. Although my parents and I were careful to mind our own business, it wasn't easy for my father to avoid looking in their direction, because of where they were sitting. Wanda's husband started giving Dad the finger and mouthing the words "fuck off." To avoid any further trouble and embarrassment, my mother suggested that we get up and leave the restaurant. On the way out, Wanda's husband kept up with his appalling behaviour. In our vehicle, we passed them again driving through the parking lot to leave the mall, and he did the same thing again, this time actually shouting the words. It was as though he was trying to provoke my father into starting a fight with him.

I would not agree to corroborate the story that Wanda planned to present to the courts, even though she was trying to scare me about the difficulties I might face upon being sent home. Rather than succumb to her pressure tactics and ultimately make matters worse, I stuck to my guns and chose to go home. Immediately after our conversation, that's exactly where she dropped me off.

During the time I spent at home with my parents, a man representing the Ministry of Social Services and Housing came to see us regarding the complaints my parents had made to the Ministry's office in Victoria. He claimed to be genuinely concerned about the complaints and asked my parents' permission to take me out for a pop so he could talk to me privately about some of the incidents that had occurred to me in care. His concerned attitude suddenly changed when we got to McDonald's. He talked about my sexual assault in the group home as if it was no big deal. In fact, he tried to make it sound as if it had never happened. He told me that it would only be a matter of time before my father abused me again. He also made it clear that the Ministry would not be so quick to help me again unless I agreed to write a letter absolving the Ministry, its employees and their contract service suppliers, of any responsibility for the abuse and the sexual assault that had occurred while I was in their care.

This ministry representative, an adult whom I guess I was supposed to trust, had me feeling very intimidated, confused and hurt. What fourteen-year-old would know what to do? My parents were sitting at home thinking that the Ministry took their complaints seriously enough to investigate them, when that was not true. This man produced a pen and a pad of paper and began to dictate to me exactly what I should write. He had me write that I did not, nor would I ever, at any future time, hold my social worker or the Minister of Social Services and Housing responsible for my being sexually assaulted or for any other abuse I suffered while I was a temporary ward of the court and (apparently) in need of their protection, under the Family and Child Services Act. After I'd finished writing the statement, he dropped me back home. Neither my parents or I ever heard from him again.

Actually, I guess I shouldn't have been too surprised by that. We heard from family friends who worked for the Ministry that all the social workers and supervisors who had any involvement with my case or our family had been reassigned. Some were transferred to other offices in other communities and others were given different assignments. I also learned that our family represented one of the Ministry's biggest cases—at the time. In Prince George, there wasn't a lawyer or Ministry worker who hadn't heard about it. A number of lawyers and supervisors from other government departments in Prince George quietly contacted me and my family, and some of the people suggested that I should make it my top priority to sue for damages as soon as I was of legal age. One or two lawyers offered their services and suggested I might like to contact them when I turned nineteen.

As I was not yet fifteen, and nineteen still seemed a long way away, any legal action of that sort would have to wait. For the time being, it was simply nice to be home with my sisters again. Mary and Ruthies' social workers had been ordered by the courts to send them home several months earlier, as no good reason had been found to keep them in care. Even though we were all at home again, family life was never the same for any of us. As a family, we never openly discussed how our lives had changed as a result of us kids being taken into care. We had been away from each other for a sufficient length of time that we were a bit uneasy, as if we had forgotten how to feel or be around one another. And this proved to be a very painful experience for us all.

I couldn't help but notice that my sisters' spirits and personalities had changed. I'm sure they felt the same way about me. The closeness and playfulness we once shared was not there, and both Mary and Ruthie acted as if they resented one another and me. Mary seemed very distant and would not talk about her experiences. Ruth, on the other hand, was an emotional wreck. She cried all the time and was very afraid the Ministry would take her away again. None of us could give back to her the security and peace she had once felt at home. Her horrifying memories of abuse in care haunted her so much that she lay awake at night, afraid to fall asleep.

When I heard about my sisters' pain, I focused less on my own similar experiences. Shortly after I had first been separated from them, they were placed into separate homes too and had been unable to contact one another. Ruthie had been sexually assaulted and harassed many times in one of her foster homes and Mary had been physically abused in a home located so far in the bush that they were only serviced by radiophone. Her foster parents would wake her up very early to dig what they led her to believe was her own grave. They told her there was no point in trying to run away because the grizzly bears would get her. Both Mary and Ruth have many horrible memories of their experiences in care—memories that haunt them still.

At that time, though, it seemed there was still hope. Things would get better again now that we were all at home. Life was indeed good for a while. I found I was getting back into the swing of things, getting reacquainted with my old friends, and having fun. I was also looking at and becoming more comfortable around boys my own age. I wanted to believe I was in charge of my own life. Unfortunately, these feelings didn't last very long. I had been offered an opportunity to go on a two-month modelling tour to Japan and I had also been contacted several times by an Ontario-based magazine to model for them while attending school out there. I was content to be back with my friends and going to high school, and I'd lost some of my earlier interest in leading the life of a model. I think I disappointed my parents by passing up on these opportunities.

My father desperately wanted to prove he was a good father, but he often tried too hard. One day he would let me wear makeup, and the next he would change his mind. Some nights he would allow me to stay out until eleven o'clock, and on other nights I'd have to be home by nine. He was also openly judgmental about many of my friends. He acted as though it was his right to choose my friends for me. Before long, the lack of communication between the two of us became a real problem. I remember my mother telling him to take it easy and leave me alone, and not follow me around and badger me about my life.

Though I didn't understand, nor could I have explained it at the time, in hindsight I understand that Dad wanted to be the father he remembered being to the cheerful young daughter he once had—and I wasn't that child anymore. My innocence was gone. He didn't realize that with all the bitterness and unhappiness and confusion I had inside me, I was no longer, nor could I or pretend to be, that little girl. Dad only remembered me as the little girl who loved the world she saw through innocent eyes. But I had learned to mistrust and hate a lot of adults. My mother often had to intervene when my father and I ended up slugging it out with one another.

When Wanda sent me home—because I wouldn't corroborate her account of what she believed had taken place in our family—she had attempted to intimidate me by saying that the Ministry would never help me again, even if I found myself in need of protection from my father. As a consequence of this, whenever my father and I got into fights, I knew I had to defend myself from his abuse instead of simply taking it—no one else was coming to my rescue. Instead of being in fear of my father, I was able to respond with my own anger. For every punch, kick or slap he gave me, I would give him one back. On one occasion, things got so out of hand that he kicked me out of the house, even though he knew that the Ministry wouldn't help me anymore. He thought this would break me—but it didn't. I was glad to leave and went to live with friends.

After a couple of weeks, Dad realized his strategy hadn't worked and he came by my friend's house to try and bring me home, acting as though nothing had ever happened between us. We were able to laugh together about the whole incident and we came to a mutual agreement—that both of us would work on being in more regular contact with each other regarding my life, the kinds of friends I chose to hang out with, and the places we went. Dad promised he would try and give me more space to be a teenager. Dad promised he would also try to set aside some of his fear of losing me again—whether it was to the government, the world, or to the resentment he felt because of all that had happened to our family during our involvement with Social Services. Unfortunately, this "truce" only lasted a very short time. I could see that the resentment he still carried had a far more powerful hold over him than anything else. It was easier for him to act out his anger toward me, because I think he saw me as the cause of it all. I was beginning to understand what Wanda had meant when she talked about my father's inability to be "forgiving" toward me. In that respect, she had been right. The older I got, the more I began to see how much alike my father and I were—headstrong and stubborn at times—and this played a big part in our continuing clashes and conflicts with one another. The recent past and our involvement with the Ministry were eating away at him, and he felt I was to blame. We were always rehashing this, along with other issues in the past, such as my relationship with my grade seven teacher, Mr. McIntosh. My mother's health had deteriorated and she wasn't strong enough to play referee anymore. Since my father would frequently get carried away during our battles, I ended up running away on a regular basis, till he cooled off, sometimes staying at a friend's house for a day or two or even a week at a time. When I received news that he had simmered down, I would always end up coming home again. This pattern of falling out and uneasy truces between us became the norm and it was never too long before the quiet moments came to an end.

I knew there was little point in my phoning the Ministry. But my friends' parents knew what was going on in my life, and they became concerned about my safety and well being. Having seen my bruises and bleeding veins, they began phoning and registering their concerns with the Ministry. During one two-week stay with friends, my friend's parents actually phoned the Ministry every day for the duration of my stay in their home. Finally, the Ministry stepped in and I was apprehended for a second time.

9

Back in Foster Care

May 5, 1987 – May 1988

On May 5, 1987, I was dispatched to yet another new foster home, twenty minutes south of Prince George. My new foster family was extremely nice. They had three of their own children, the youngest of whom was just six months old when I arrived. I spent every free moment I had with them, or riding the horses the family kept at their home in the country. In the six months I stayed with them, they took me everywhere with them. I was included in long family vacations, visits to grandma's house in Vanderhoof, as well as the ordinary life events like trips to the local park and even to the grocery store. While I was living with them, I started to focus on my hobbies again. I became very involved in my modern ballet and jazz dance lessons and would cycle a round-trip of more than fifty kilometres between their house and town, in order to attend my dance classes. It took me some time to allow myself to trust these people—I was so afraid of being rejected. Both Lester and Lorraine are a very important influence and continued presence in my life.

I was also assigned a good social worker, Samantha, who was genuinely concerned about me and my family. Samantha either visited me or called me at least once a week—to see how I was doing and to offer me encouragement. In her words, my family situation represented "nothing but a political case." She believed that there were no protection concerns for my life, but that there was a serious need for in-depth counselling to rebuild unity within my family. She made her feelings and opinions known, and documented these beliefs in writing. Her main goal, she said, was to help me rebuild my relationship with my family so that I could return home under better conditions. In the meantime, if I couldn't be at home with my parents, then this new foster home was the next best thing.

It seemed almost too good to be true that I would have her as my social worker. Then, after about four or five weeks, she was removed from my case. Samantha explained to me that she felt she had done her best to represent me and look out for my best interests, as well as those of my family. I cried, both in fear and disbelief, and begged her to challenge her reassignment and take the matter as high as the offices of the Superintendent of Family and Child Services in Victoria, if she had to. Apparently, Samantha had already done this and had met with little success. "You are at the centre of a very political and volatile case," she reminded me. I didn't really understand what Samantha meant but she reassured me that she would keep tabs on me, and she was as good as her word—continuing to stay in touch with me and, in a quiet and unobtrusive way, even visit me from time to time.

She also told my foster parents, Lester and Lorraine, that they were the best thing for my life, and she was right. Many other children who were "fostered" in this family feel as I do toward Lester and Lorraine, and a number of us have remained in contact with them over the years. Lester and Lorraine have become parents to many children, and their own children have come to love many brothers and sisters. I am afraid to think about the direction my life might have taken without them. Before I came to their home, I was on a trajectory that would have likely seen me on the streets. It's perfectly conceivable that I'd have ended up with a group of other foster girls my age, prostituting myself as a means of staying out of the hands of the monster known to us as the Ministry of Social Services and Housing. A girl I met while in care subsequently died of AIDS, which she acquired while working as a prostitute. She left three children behind. Some foster girls have been or are presently in jail. A few have committed suicide. Many others are just lost to the streets, the only world that seemed to accept them and populated by others with whom they may have experienced some measure of understanding. If I were to speculate, I think I would have ended up among those who attempted and sometimes succeed in suicide. I think I would have attempted to take my own life out of self-loathing and disgust over all the pain and suffering I experienced and witnessed while living in care. I contemplated suicide, but I survived, knowing that I could put an end to my suffering at any time, knowing I could choose not to see or feel any more of it.

After Samantha was reassigned, I was given a new social worker, Connie, who was just twenty-three years old. I was also assigned to a childcare worker, Pamela, who was, as far as I was concerned, completely immature and irresponsible, and should never have been assigned to someone of my age. I dreaded the few hours I had to spend with her each week. Our sessions were supposed to represent quality time for me, but she was too busy following men around town and spying on them. Apparently, she had dated some of these men just once, but they hadn't called her back for a second date. Her routine would involve parking her car a block away, but in plain view of the residence of one of her acquaintances. I would be forced to sit with her in the car, often for more than an hour at a time, while she hoped to see one of her ex-dates show up—either arriving or departing the stake-out! Pamela talked incessantly about her debts and how much money she owed all over town and I began to think that she, more than I, was the one in need of some kind of care.

In October of 1987 I met Stefan, who had come to Canada from West Germany the previous year in order to live with his father. He was a breath of fresh air in my life, and we became very close after only one month of dating. Stefan became my freedom, my protection and my voice. With him, I found another world in which to escape some of the more difficult aspects of my own predicament. Pamela pushed and pushed for me to set her up with Stefan's father; she had met him once and decided that he was wealthy. Though I felt like an idiot, I told Stefan that Pamela was interested in his father. Eventually, with the help of Lester and Lorraine, who believed Pamela to be a bad influence on me, I succeeded in having my appointments with her curtailed and henceforth kept her out of my life.

Six months after I'd moved into this good foster home, the Ministry of Social Services & Housing accused Lester and Lorraine of providing too much for me and being too generous materially. The Ministry's solution was to move me into yet another foster home. My sister Mary was also back in foster care, and Lester and Lorraine, who had repeatedly requested my return, said they would take the two of us so we could be together. Connie had also become Mary's case worker, and had claimed my sisters were being sexually abused at home—the reason why they had been apprehended again. While Connie said she hadn't been able to confirm who was abusing them, she was sure the abuse was taking place. Connie had tried unsuccessfully to apprehend Ruth. Thus far, Ruth had run away and hidden herself every time Connie or the protection team had showed up at home. No one knew where she was, and she would stay in hiding for days at a time. Ruth was clearly determined that the Ministry was never going to put her back in care.

Of course, after repeatedly investigating Connie's allegations, the RCMP continued to disagree that any of us were ever sexually abused in our home and they would not pursue the matter further or press charges. Instead, they were "leaving matters in the hands of MSS&H." Nevertheless, the Ministry presented their allegations of sexual abuse in court as both a defence for our apprehension and as a reason for why we should be kept in care.

Connie was very upset at the lack of cooperation on the part of my parents. Mom and Dad found it very difficult to work with a social worker who was so young, especially one who had never been married or had her own children, and who was, herself, the product of a broken home—something which she freely discussed. There were times when Connie would try to engage the assistance of the police in her attempts to enter my parents' home, having accused my mother and father of ignoring her calls. Apparently, the police responded by demanding that Connie stay off my parents' property. This infuriated her to the point that she would go to the edge of my parents' lawn—the property line, and scream and jump up and down, as a child would do in the midst of a temper tantrum.

I couldn't understand why the Ministry would take me away from a foster family I was happy with, and who seemed to like having me in their home. I was always included as one of their family. They shared so much with me. The party they gave me for my sixteenth birthday still stands out as one of the best parties I've ever had. It was just the six of us, a big cake decorated with beautiful flowers, and so many gifts for me that I felt like a well-loved teen.

We spent many hours talking, laughing and sharing with one another. Lester and Lorraine gave to me as they gave to their own children—out of the goodness of their hearts. Any money they received from the Ministry for my care was spent on me or given to me for my own use. Lester and Lorraine received just over $300 a month for my care, but this barely covered the extent of the real costs of my living with them. Through their unselfish love and patience, I learned once again how to trust, love and respect myself and others. Lester and Lorraine helped me to restore my will and rediscover the free spirit I thought I'd lost forever.

Although the Ministry tried to put a stop to it, I continued to visit them regularly, long after I was placed in my new foster home. In this new home, I was nowhere near as happy as I had been for the previous six months. Because of the level of stress and emotional turmoil in my life, my menstrual cycle had become erratic and I was prescribed birth control pills as a means of regulating my periods. I experienced some side effects to the hormones but was required to take them anyway, even though I was not and had never been sexually active. I gained weight, putting on nearly thirty pounds in less than two months. The only comfort I found, to help cope with the stress of everything in my life, was writing in my journal—especially poetry. I wrote something close to one hundred poems examining my life and, for a while, the only time I felt in sync with the rational world was when I was writing a poem or short story.

The Ministry believed that my continuing contact with Lester and Lorraine and their family was causing my depression and weight gain, and keeping me from settling into my new home. Worst of all, they accused Lester and Lorraine of undermining my development. The Ministry said Lester and Lorraine had merely picked up where my own parents had left off way back when I had first been apprehended in December of 1985. The Ministry felt I had always been given too much in the way of hygiene products, clothes or whatever they chose as gifts or rewards in return for my babysitting or the other chores I elected to undertake. The Ministry also accused Lester and Lorraine of emotionally abusing me by expressing their genuine care for me as a child in their home, treating me as if I were their own. In fact, Lester and Lorraine were the first foster parents I ever had who actually advocated for me and genuinely looked out for my best interests with regard to the Ministry and its involvement in my life.

I was very confused by the position the Ministry chose to adopt with Lester and Lorraine. It had been so difficult for me to develop a sense of trust and belonging, and finally feel safe. Having achieved this level of security, it was as though I had done something wrong and was being punished for it, especially when Connie threatened me that if the new foster home didn't work out for me, she would have me placed in a group home. She mentioned the name of a group home that every foster child in Prince George feared. The thought of another group home horrified me, and I let her know clearly that I would kill myself before I would stay in a group home. She told me that would be my choice. Lester and Lorraine had helped me feel positive about myself and my life with them. But I'd had enough experiences with abuse, manipulation and neglect in foster homes to know that I couldn't trust anyone who worked for the Ministry.

I had felt safe with Lester and Lorraine, protected not only from abuse, neglect and manipulation, but most importantly, from the Ministry and all that came with it. The Ministry was also aware that I did not trust anyone on their staff. I only feared their power.

10

Moved Again

May 1988 - May 1989

I was transferred to another foster home in the downtown bowl. Once again I was placed with a single mother, Lydia—who worked with schizophrenics and had a son, Mitch, only a few days older than me. Things started out well enough. I was still seeing Stefan and going to school on a regular basis, and I was very excited about winning one of thirteen spots in the Miss Prince George Teen Pageant as more than two hundred girls had applied.

To qualify for the pageant, one had to have good grades in school, be respected by both ones' teachers and peers, and be involved in some sort of community service. Contestants also had to be judged as possessing the kind of reputation, attitudes, and personality deemed appropriate for someone destined to represent the City of Prince George in the Miss Teen Canada Pageant.

Although it was against the rules, both Connie and Pamela decided they would help me out with my speeches—and I really didn't have much choice! I grew frustrated with their efforts and annoyed about all of their overt references to my being in foster care and the extent of the financial assistance the Ministry had provided me, in the way of clothing and accessories, to support my participation in the competition.

During the early stages of the competition, I felt I had done quite well. I later learned that I had done so well in the preliminary rounds, I had accumulated more points than any other previous contestant had ever achieved.

Devastatingly, success eluded me that night. Connie had repeatedly reminded me about the extent of the support I had received and burdened me with the expectations of others—and I was not to let the Ministry down. I lost my temper and expressed my anger towards Connie—an outburst witnessed by others and resulted in my being disqualified. While I was permitted to complete the evening, this was only because there were people who had paid to come to see me among the record-breaking crowd of what had been a sold-out show. While stubborn pride kept me going through most of the evening, my disappointment at being disqualified eventually overwhelmed me and I broke down in tears, on stage, in front of all those hundreds of people. I had been a contender, poised to win, but had ended up with nothing more than an increased sense of failure, sadness and a further wound to my self-esteem.

Though I was continuing at school, I'd lost much interest after I was reapprehended. I felt so overwhelmed that I dreaded the thought of going to school. It didn't help that I began to have health problems. After running many tests, the doctors discovered that my white blood cell count was extremely high. I caught every virus going around and suffered constantly from infections of various kinds. I was even rushed to hospital for exploratory surgery for what the doctors referred to as "very serious concerns." In my family, I knew there was a history of ovarian cancer, sometimes beginning at a very early age.

Fortunately, the problem was not ovarian cancer, nor anything quite so serious. When I was well enough to be released from hospital, a social worker took me to a group home called Dogwood Street (which was a girls-only resource). My sister Mary was living here along with maybe five other girls. My presence was supposed to be temporary, although I would stay for two weeks before returning to live with Lydia and Mitch.

Including overnight, short-term and emergency placements, Dogwood Street was my fourteenth placement since first being apprehended, and it was truly awful. While I was staying at Dogwood Street, Lydia began phoning and leaving messages for me with Stefan—basically to grant her permission for me to stay over on weekends at his house, with Stefan and his father. I didn't mind this arrangement, but it also seemed to me that Lydia wanted the money more than she wanted to take care of me. That she wasn't very welcoming of my presence in her home made me realize the extent of my domestic instability.

The group home parents, Monty and Tara, tried their best to keep Mary and me apart and wouldn't allow us to share a bedroom. They clearly didn't like Mary because she had recently taken up with a religion that lived strictly by the Bible and did not acknowledge or celebrate any worldly or "pagan" holidays. When they were unsuccessful in their attempts to distract her from her Bible studies, they began making life very difficult for her in any other way they could think of. At every meal, they would give her a portion of food only half the size they gave everyone else. Since the portions were already based on "health regulation" sizes—usually only a quarter to one half that of a normal restaurant portion—Mary went to bed at night crying simply because she was hungry. I complained about this, but the group home parents turned on me, sending me to my room for the rest of the day.

Occasionally Monty and Tara took all of us with them to a donut shop in town. They would order a big lunch for themselves, along with donuts and pop, then eat it all in front of us, explaining that according to the Health Board we were not allowed to eat this kind of food. The girls who were living at Dogwood Street became so desperate that, if they weren't running away, they were stealing and hiding food under their beds.

On weekdays, Monty would drive Mary and me to school, since our schools were much too far away for either of us to walk. Monty would drive me almost to the door of my school. However, as a way of picking on Mary and undermining not just her beliefs but our relationship as siblings, he would drop her off on the other side of town and make her get out and walk to school. By the time she got there, she would be late and cold and, of course, upset.

On my last night in the group home, I broke the rules and spent the night with Mary in her room. We snuggled up together in her bed, not wanting to be separated again. Although I planned to wake up early and return to my room so we wouldn't get caught, we both slept in. Monty and Tara were very angry to discover that Mary and I had spent a night together, and neither of us were allowed to have breakfast.

Monty yelled at us all the way to school, calling us "a couple of tramps" and "sneaking, fucking bitches." Both of us were still a long way from our respective schools when he pulled the car over. "Get out of my fucking car!," he screamed.

He was in such a hurry for us to get out of the car that he squealed his tires before I had been able to get clear of the vehicle. As he pulled away, I stumbled, tripped and fell, placing all my weight on an outstretched hand, and hyperextended my wrist. "I'd better not see your face again," he threatened me as he took off. I still have problems with this wrist today.

I walked with Mary as far as my own school, but she still had another three or four kilometres to go. I was so shocked by what had happened that I wanted to talk to my teachers about it. As usual, I was afraid they wouldn't believe me. I was also afraid to go back to the group home after school and see how Mary was doing. When I tried to call her later that evening, Monty or Tara would answer and, when they found out it was me, they would just hang up the phone. Monty was well known by the girls for his violent behaviour. I heard later that he got physically abusive with one of the girls in the group home, and she ended up in a juvenile detention home for defending herself. Anyone who lived at Dogwood Street during the tenure of Monty and Tara would have witnessed their abusive behaviour; many of us actually suffered at their hands; some former residents continue to live with the consequences of that abuse.

Sometimes, Mary was able to sneak out to call me or drop by my foster home to see me, but these were never heartwarming visits. She would cry with me that Monty and Tara were starving her. I felt so sorry for her that I would send her home with groceries I stole from my foster home. I could hardly eat myself, I was so worried that she wasn't eating properly.

My interest in attending school had further declined and I was so far behind, I decided to quit altogether. I got myself a full-time job at a convenience store and spent the rest of my time with Stefan. Other than returning to sleep, I spent hardly any time at all at Lydia's place. Although the Ministry paid Lydia about $400 a month, on regular foster care rates, to look after me, she approached the Ministry and complained that this wasn't enough. As a Mental Health employee, she didn't think it was fair that she had to go to work all day only to come home and continue her work with me. She asked the Ministry to pay her more money—an additional $707 per month. The Ministry agreed to her request, out of some conviction that Lydia was spending a lot of time with me and perhaps providing me with some sort of therapy. Apparently, she even demanded a support payment each month for Pippy, and when the Ministry mistakenly issued her a monthly cheque in an amount that was twelve dollars less than agreed, she was quickly on the phone demanding they rectify the error.

There came a time during my placement with Lydia that I realized I'd simply had enough of the Ministry dictating and controlling my life. With the money I made by working full-time, I began to buy and store everything I thought I would need in order to move out on my own the day I turned seventeen. My plan was to have my job cut back to half-time, return to finish my schooling, and take whatever additional education I needed to become self-employed and be my own boss. When I shared my plans with Connie and Lydia, they tried to discourage me, telling me I was living in a fantasy world and that I was being completely unrealistic about living on my own so soon. They said I was a dreamer.

I waited impatiently for my seventeenth birthday. When that day came, even though Connie and Lydia had seen everything I had collected to be ready to go out on my own, they still didn't believe I was going to do it. Connie sat me down with Lydia and told me that my temporary wardship had expired. If I didn't want to go home to my parents, I would have to pay Lydia rent. Little did they know I had already rented and furnished an apartment! All I had to do was take the rest of my boxes and move in. Connie didn't believe I would stick to my goals and became furious with me. But there was nothing she could do about it. My mind was set.

On May 4, 1989, not quite two months after my seventeenth birthday, I was finally released from care. It felt wonderful to be out on my own. A week later, I qualified for my driver's license and registered in school to complete my grade twelve. From there, I went on to obtain my license as a cosmetologist. Out of concern for others, particularly very young foster children living in care, I applied to become a foster parent myself. I hoped to give a couple of kids a decent home with me, to avoid the horrors I had gone through when I was in care. Since I wasn't yet of age, the Ministry rejected my application although I was encouraged to apply again when I was older.

11

Life After Foster Care

May 1989 - Present

When I say that growing up in the care of the Ministry almost destroyed me, I am telling the truth. Every dream I had for my life, every goal I ever planned for my future was thrown back in my face by abusive foster parents and inept social workers who didn't believe in me. I was constantly told that my dreams were fantasy. But they seemed simple and real enough to me—I wanted to move out on my own, finish school, and hold down a full-time job. Someday, I wanted to be my own boss, to own a business and pursue something I was both good at and enjoyed. These were not fantasies. They were reasonable hopes for any young person. In fact, by the time I was twenty years old I had accomplished all of these things and much, much more.

After finishing grade twelve and some post-secondary studies through distance education, I obtained my certification as a cosmetologist and started my own business in Prince George. I married Stefan, and we had two children. My son, Bruno, was born in 1991 and a daughter, Brittany, in 1994. By 1995, at the age of twenty-three, I was beginning to suffer from my years in foster homes. So much had happened to me in such a short time, from 1985 - 1989, that I knew I had to face my foster-home experiences instead of running from them.

I was under so much stress that I needed to take some time out and went to visit my Aunt Marlene, Uncle Leonard and my cousins in the USA. I had arranged for a nanny to help Stefan look after Bruno and Brittany, who was ten months old at the time. One afternoon, when she was supposed to be napping, Brittany managed to crawl into the bathroom, fall into the tub and turn on the hot water tap. The scalding water caused life-threatening, third degree burns to approximately seventeen per cent of her body, and she required skin grafts. I came home immediately to be with her.

On top of all this, the happy, peaceful life I had hoped for with Stefan was not to be. His abuse and manipulation of some of his closest family members against me threw me into a world of darkness. I was blamed for my daughter's accident and accused of being selfish for leaving my husband and daughter.

I was truly lost. I had no one to talk to about the distressing issues in my life—the abuse I had suffered while in care was always with me. I agreed to go for an assessment and was diagnosed by a psychiatrist as suffering from Post-Traumatic Stress Disorder, the result of the abuse, and prescribed medications to relieve some of the stress and reduce the toll it was taking on my health. My life was out of control. I gave up my job and my business and lost my spirit. I had no will to carry on. The negativity from my past and the present dilemma I was facing left me feeling lost and hopeless. My relationship with Stefan and his family had deteriorated to such a degree that I realized I had simply moved on from abusive situations in care to yet another one where I was manipulated, controlled, and abused.

It's easier to read about Post-Traumatic Stress Disorder than to live with it. At any given moment, I would be flooded with vivid memories of specific incidents of the abuse I had suffered while I was in care. I didn't even have to think about these things consciously. They would just rush into my mind, usually unexpectedly, and often when I was feeling relaxed and happy. I would feel a smile coming to my lips, then be jolted by a haunting memory that left me emotional, sensitive and depressed. I believe the migraine headaches I suffered were also caused by the stress related to my flashbacks. These flashbacks lasted only a few seconds, but they brought with them a million words, filling my head with thoughts I couldn't escape.

One of the memories that came to me repeatedly was of Jenny—the face of the tearful little girl I had found attempting to hang herself. Once, when I was driving, this event came to my mind so suddenly and vividly, I almost drove into the ditch.

Another frequently recurring memory came in the form of a frightening dream that continued night after night as if it were a television serial, always picking up right where it left off. In this dream, I see myself running between the thick and twisted trunks of an ancient forest, being chased by faceless, nameless people who are wearing black cloaks. While I am running, I am wishing that I could die. Though I run as fast as I can, these faceless phantoms are always close behind me. My pursuers seem to glide over the ground. This particular dream began when I was about fifteen, stopped for about a year, and then returned and recurred more frequently until I was about twenty-two.

I had no idea why I was experiencing these sorts of symptoms, but I was reluctant to let these flashbacks and nightmares rob me of anymore of my life energy. My birth family didn't really understand what had happened to me, nor did they try very hard to show they wanted to understand, and I couldn't blame them—my sisters had enough demons of their own to live with. I tried to appear as normal and stable as possible, but I no longer felt I had any clear sense of Self. Instead, I learned to shape myself to be whatever a situation required of me. If I needed to be seen and not heard, I would be quiet. If I needed to serve, I would become a servant. This helped me to keep my sanity and pride intact.

Eventually, my own family did come through for me and rescued me. I left Stefan and his immediate family in Prince George, and my parents brought me and my two children home with them to Nanaimo, on Vancouver Island. Once there, they nourished me with love as they had done in my early childhood, and I was able to regain my health, my free spirit, and my will. I found beauty inside myself again and felt ready to face the ugly world of my past back in Prince George. After two years of living in peace with my family I was at last able to let go of a lot of what had happened to me in care. I felt stable enough to be back on my own. With the help of my family, I had found a way to set myself free.

Today, I believe I should never have been placed in foster care. I feel strongly that if my sisters and I had needed protection from our father, the Ministry could have taken a vastly different approach. For starters, they could have required my father to leave the family home, instead of us kids, mandated some form of counselling for anger management, and given him some new skills and tools to discipline his children more appropriately. By taking us away from him, the Ministry provoked the situation, and my father became less able to control his temper and more prone to outbursts of anger than before they entered our lives and broke up our family. There were never any problems with alcohol, drugs, or firearms, nor anything remotely approaching sexual abuse—nothing other than our father's old-fashioned methods of discipline. The Ministry was callous and heavy-handed with our family. They ended our life together and gave very little thought to our well being.

Over these interim years, I have rebuilt a relationship with my family; yet nothing will ever return to us or make up for the lost and wasted years. Forgiveness can be hard, forgetting nearly impossible, but time has a way of closing wounds.

When I look back at the sexual assault, an experience that has left me emotionally scarred to this day, I now understand that Raymond was also a victim. Not only was he abused by the system that placed him in a situation where he would be likely to offend again, but he was also placed inappropriately in a home managed by well-meaning but inadequately trained or qualified caregivers. Caroline and Lawrence despised Ray from day one because he came from a home where personal hygiene was neither taught nor practiced. He was considered filthy and disgusting because he had to be told to bathe or take a shower. Instead of spending quality time with him, Lawrence would easily lose patience with him, and end up undermining any relationship he might have built with Ray, succeeding only in making him feel less important than the other foster children. There was also a lot of inappropriate, judgmental and critical discussion about Ray. Caroline and Lawrence constantly drew unnecessary and unfair comparisons between Ray and the other children, openly talking about his offensive lack of personal hygiene, and questioning his masculinity. When it came time to help Lawrence with chores that required strength, Ray was criticized—hardly a therapeutic environment.

On several occasions, Ray was caught stalking children in malls, parks and streets and on school grounds. He was still below the age of majority, and acted out like a child in need of some serious professional help. The people who were ultimately in charge of our care ignored many warning signs—including signs that I was in danger of being molested by this boy. When alerted to the situation by the group home parents, the Ministry failed to provide the backup support and the timely intervention that was required.

I often think about Ray and the other foster children I met during my time in care. I especially remember some of the many girls of native ancestry who lived with me. They were no different from the rest of us but they were still called "dirty Indians." Many of them will bear the scars of their physical abuse and neglect for the rest of their lives—and these are only the scars we can see. The hidden scars of sexual, emotional, and psychological abuse are often much worse.

My memories of these girls haunt me particularly because of the secret I kept to spare myself further pain. My grandfather, an Ojibwa from the Garden River Nation, was born on a reservation. My father is half-Native, and I am proud of this part of my ancestry, but I was always afraid it would become known while I was in the care of the Ministry. I knew that life was often much harder for Native children than it had ever been for me.

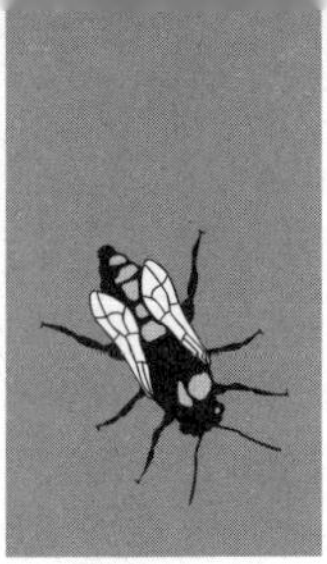

Epilogue

The Future?

In 1998, along with a number of others who had lived in care, I approached the RCMP. We wanted to verify our own beliefs that we had grounds to press charges against those who abused us when we were foster children. Based on our disclosures, a criminal investigation was started and, with the media coverage that followed, other victims have also found the courage to come forward.

Shortly thereafter, I began to receive phone calls from various provincial government offices and from the President of the B.C. Federation of Foster Parent Associations. While I was a foster child, I learned to document key conversations and record everything accurately so that I would be better prepared to defend myself against possible deception and manipulation. When I began receiving phone calls, I decided to record them and even disclosed to some of the callers that I was running a tape recorder.

Initially, the calls came from an Area Manager in Prince George. He explained that he was calling on behalf of the government and said that the Ministry had asked him to contact me directly. He wanted to know if I would be interested in meeting with members of the Ministry, from government offices in Victoria, for the purposes of settling my issues quietly. Previously, I had received similar calls requesting the same sort of thing from the Minister's office in Prince George.

Fifteen minutes after telling the Area Manager that I would be willing to sit down with the government, I received another phone call from Victoria. Because they had responded so quickly, I listened to what they had to say but let the answer machine take the massage. I wasn't sure I could trust them. After several more messages from Victoria, I finally took their call a few days later. The caller explained who he was, his role with the government, and that he was seeking confirmation of my willingness to meet with him, along with lawyers for the Ministry and other government stakeholders, including representatives from the Office of the Attorney General. He offered to arrange a meeting with me wherever I chose, but said it should occur within the following week.

When I suggested that I would like to have my lawyer present, he responded by saying that lawyers only complicated matters. The ministry wanted to meet with me alone. Regardless, I contacted my lawyer and asked him to intervene and help arrange this meeting with the government. After my lawyer became involved, the government sent a letter denying that they had ever contacted me or discussed meeting with me. They also stated they knew I had written a manuscript for a book and demanded that I send them a copy of the document.

Through all of these convoluted communications, I was feeling angry. I telephoned the offices of the Ministry of Social Services and Housing in Prince George, and spoke with the Area Manager who had originally contacted me on behalf of the government. He acknowledged that he had phoned me and further explained the purpose of his original calls. After disclosing to him the nature of the letter government officials in Victoria had sent to my lawyer, he insisted that his own intentions in contacting me were both good and honest. The Area Manager said he didn't know what the government in Victoria was up to, but I should believe him when he said his intentions were sincere.

That same day, I phoned the Premier's Office with a complaint related to my case. While I waited for a call back, I phoned the Prince George RCMP detachment and talked to Constable Jane Taylor. In the middle of my conversation with her, I received another incoming call and it turned out to be an Assistant to the Premier—calling on behalf of the Premier who happened to be on holiday. I put the Assistant on hold and told Constable Taylor who was on my other line.

The Premier's Assistant asked me about my complaints and what I thought the government should do about them. He was clear to point out that the government really did not care about me or my concerns. In fact, he seemed to find some humour in talking to me, and I became so angry that I hung up. For the next forty-five minutes, prank calls were made to my home, during which the Premier's Assistant talked rudely to my eight-year-old son whenever he answered the phone. When we ignored the phone, he would just let it ring and ring until we answered. Finally I phoned the RCMP again to report the harassment and unprofessional nature of his calls. When he called yet again, I answered phone and told him I had notified the RCMP. The Premier's Assistant then called my lawyer's office and left a message for him to call the Premier's Office.

I was very disturbed by this man's tone, manner and attitude. There was nothing at all amusing about what I had said to him. We were discussing child abuse and the deaths of children while in the care of the Ministry. Just a few days after our conversation, it was reported in the media that a young Native girl was found brain dead in a foster home. Her younger brother had also been injured and was in critical condition.

I was also disturbed by the response I received from the President of the B.C. Federation of Foster Parent Associations (herself a foster parent for about ten years). When I mentioned that within the Prince George area alone, nearly fifty former foster children had already come forward with complaints of abuse while in care, her response was "What are fifty against 5000?" Then she added, "What if children who were in my home ten years ago subsequently come forward and accuse me of being abusive towards them, simply because they didn't like me?" I replied that she would only need to be concerned if she were guilty of abuse.

At the time of writing, we (who disclosed to the RCMP the treatment received in foster care) are waiting for Crown Counsel to press charges against those who abused us. In many cases, this process will involve the same members of Crown Counsel who permitted us to be placed in care. Personally, I share the opinion currently held by the RCMP: that this sort of criminal investigation is only in its infancy. There are too many of us—many generations, in fact—who suffered while in foster care and other child-care resources, like group homes, by caregivers that were approved by the Ministry and supposed to protect us from further abuse.

As for the abuse in my own life, the Ministry's excuse is that it would have happened to me anyway. While this is sheer conjecture, to date it forms the basis for their belief that they have no responsibility for what happened to me while I was a ward of the court in the care of the Superintendent of Family and Child Services.

Over the years, I have had many doors slammed in my face by the Ministry, even when I begged them to act and stop the abuse my sisters and I suffered in care. Sometimes, my sisters and I are able to pick up the threads of our former lives, before we were initially apprehended, and experience the joy and the laughter we used to share. But these moments are rare, because our meetings are haunted by the memories of how we lived with pain, fear, guilt, abandonment and sorrow. After a visit, we cannot part without remembering how we were separated from each other as foster children. Now we live in different communities throughout B.C. and find our own ways of coping with the past.

Our greatest gifts, and perhaps the only important outcome of our early lives, are the children we each gave birth to when we were just teenagers ourselves. My youngest sister, Ruth, is now twenty-four. She has never been married and is the single mother of two children—the first of whom was born when she was just fourteen. Mary is now twenty-five, the single mother of one and in the midst of her second divorce. I am twenty-seven, divorced, and a single mother of two.

Many children in foster care live their lives behind a dark curtain of secrecy and silence; such curtains must be torn down. For us, my sisters and I, and for many others in north central British Columbia, the time has come to step forward and talk about our truth and our experience. Among the readers of this account, I invite those who also suffered abuse while in care to find the courage to step forward, stand with us, and reclaim our lives. We cannot change what happened to us. However, by acting on our sense of obligation towards all the children—approximately 10,000 of them, who are presently in the care of provincial governments here in British Columbia and elsewhere across Canada—we might help to break the cycle of abuse.

If we can achieve that, perhaps we will each experience a greater sense of healing, and with that a strengthened resolve to let go of our past, not by burying it, but by telling it. In bringing our own truth to light, we will do that which no one did for us: remove the curtain that hides the secrets, the silence, the darkness—the breach of trust.

Gloria May Biron
Prince George, British Columbia
December 1999